HRAFNKELS
SAGA FREYSGOÐA

A STUDY BY SIGURÐUR NORDAL

TRANSLATED BY R. GEORGE THOMAS

CARDIFF
UNIVERSITY OF WALES PRESS
1958

PRINTED IN GREAT BRITAIN

HRAFNKELS SAGA FREYSGOÐ

A STUDY

A translation of *Hrafnkatla* Íslenzk Fræði 7,
Reykjavík 1949

FOREWORD

NOT least among many reasons for offering to English readers a translation of Professor Sigurður Nordal's monograph *Hrafnkatla* is the difficulty with which most undergraduate students of Old Icelandic pick their way through it in its Modern Icelandic dress. And now that *Hrafnkels saga Freysgoða* has been included in its entirety in the second edition of Gordon's *Introduction to Old Norse* (revised by A. R. Taylor), it is more than ever necessary that Professor Nordal's classic analysis of this magnificent saga should be followed in detail. I hope the present translation will not act as a barrier between the author's sense and the reader's need of it, for I am quite certain that it cannot reproduce the stylistic grace and brimful good humour of the original.

Many scholars have generously helped me to make this translation as accurate as it is, though the finished form (and the errors) are my own. In particular I am grateful to Mr. Benedikt Benedikz and Mr. Peter G. Foote for saving my draft translations from many pitfalls which lie concealed from the unwary. My debt to Professor Gwyn Jones of Aberystwyth—himself the best translator of *Hrafnkels saga*—is more difficult to define, since his constant encouragement, ready help, and sage counsel have always been generously given; even more, I am grateful to him and to Professor E. C. Llewellyn of Cardiff (my first guides through the Icelandic sagas) for their continued friendly interest in my work. Above all, my gratitude and thanks are due to Professor Sigurður Nordal. I shall never adequately measure his many acts of kindness to me in Reykjavík when I served with H.M. Forces in Iceland, nor the ready granting of his permission to allow *Hrafnkatla* to be translated, nor, most of all, his careful comments and numerous suggestions after reading two drafts of this present translation amid the manifold cares of his public life and official duties in Copenhagen. For all such assistance this work seems quite inadequate compensation; my sincere hope is that after reading it other students of the Family Sagas will turn to the rest of Professor Nordal's published work and derive from that the inspiration and example which have sustained my own interest in Old Icelandic literature during the last two decades.

Finally and with filial affection I wish to thank the University of Wales Press Board for undertaking to publish a translation which at first sight seems far removed from its special interests. The country which can boast *The Four Branches of the Mabinogi* among its treasured literary heritage has long fostered Norse studies in its colleges and maintained a constant watch on the interaction of Northern and Celtic literary forces. The publication of this translation is one further proof of the interest taken in Wales in the cultural heritage of the Modern Icelandic Republic.

R. GEORGE THOMAS

University College,
  Cardiff

CONTENTS

	FOREWORD	v
I	THE THEME	1
II	HISTORICAL TRUTHFULNESS	7
III	SOURCES	27
IV	COMPOSITION AND METHOD OF NARRATION	34
V	CHARACTERIZATION	46
VI	FINDINGS AND CONCLUSIONS	56
	NOTES	68

I
THE THEME

THIS monograph has its own history and I think that its aim will become clearer if I explain how it was written and why it is being published now.

I had read *Hrafnkatla*,[1] as I had read other Icelandic sagas, with great pleasure as a boy; yet it was only when I re-read it with ripened judgement that I first realized what a remarkable work of art it was. I had, of course, no doubts that the saga owed its final form and finish to an author, but at that time I had not conducted independent research into the Icelandic sagas, and so I did not bother myself with trying to discover how it had been shaped. I was content to enjoy the saga for its own sake and to stimulate interest in its quality—particularly abroad where it had not received the attention it deserved. For instance, I read through this saga in the autumn of 1925 with a small group of Norse scholars at Oslo and later helped towards its publication in a convenient edition for foreign university students.[2]

Since P. E. Muller's first article on the saga in Sagabibliothek I in 1817 and Konráð Gíslason's preface to the first edition of it in 1839, it has been accounted one of the most reliable of the Icelandic sagas; Guðbrandur Vigfússon, Finnur Jónsson, and Bogi Th. Melsteð have trusted to it more than to *Landnáma* when the two sources differed. F. S. Cawley is not overstating the case when he writes in the introduction to his edition: '*Hrafnkels saga* is generally acknowledged to be one of the best of the whole group in faithfulness to historical fact', &c. Side by side with this generally accepted view went the belief that after being shaped from old and accurate traditions the saga was committed to writing early and, in the process, was little altered by the saga-writer. Along with *Glúms saga* and *Heiðarvíga saga* Heusler includes it among the 'definitely early redactions' which show 'that for the most part the essential saga style had already been formed when quill was put to vellum'. He thinks it quite possible that the saga had been told to audiences outside the district where its events had occurred: 'We need not believe that the gripping story of the fate of Hrafnkel godi, his fall and restoration, had for nearly 250 years been known and cherished by the people of Jǫkulsdalr and Fljótsdalr alone.'[3] Liestøl indeed admits that the saga bears some traces of a writer (in his delight, for example, in the study of place-names), but, compared with *Njála*, *Laxdœla*, and *Egla*, he reckons it among the more 'impersonal sagas'.[4] E. V. Gordon says: 'Sagas such as *Hrafnkels saga* and *Bandamanna saga* were probably complete unities before they were written down, and cannot have been much altered as stories by the men who first put them into writing'.[5] Paasche, it is true, states that the saga cannot be unchanged from the one which was told in the tenth century and that the art of the story-tellers has somewhat encroached on the historical truth, but he adds: 'The finished product of superior art need not be attributed to an author, since the texts show few clear signs of his activities.'[6] These opinions are quite representative of the views of scholars about the historical accuracy of the saga and its origins.

At first glance it seems no easy task to question the truthfulness of the events recounted in *Hrafnkatla*. Few sources are available for direct comparison. The events in the saga are presented clearly and without exaggeration. There are no stories about trolls, ghosts, or second sight; no extravagant tales about the fantastic deeds of Icelanders abroad; no distinct traces of influences from foreign stories nor indeed from other Icelandic sagas. The whole story is presented to us with the confident assurance that the incidents had taken place in just this way: the events form an organic whole, answering at once the demands of reason and nature. Mere suspicions are of little value in dealing with such a work unless the dissecting knife can probe into and discover some vulnerable spot.

Many years ago it occurred to me to try to make a closer study of the power and authority of the sons of Thjóstarr by analysing what other sources said about individuals and families in the Vestfirðir: the results will be set out in this monograph. It then became clear to me that not only was *Hrafnkatla* an extremely entertaining saga but that it would repay a detailed analysis. I seemed to hold a loose thread in my hand and gradually the whole saga was unravelled—not only the value of the historical subject-matter it contained, but the very shape and form into which the saga had been fashioned, Ever since, I have constantly had it in mind, delivering lectures on it at home and abroad, studying it closely with my students, and discussing it with a number of my colleagues. Many of them will find nothing new here; but although it was completed many years ago, the results of this investigation, like so many other ideas and notions about the Family Sagas, have been left to mature at the bottom of a drawer.

There is a special reason why I have now decided to touch it up and place it before the public. Recently I have finished a brief survey of the old Icelandic sagas which has now (1956) appeared in *Nordisk Kultur*.[7] In that survey I have had to make statements about the dating and origin of the sagas which I believe to be correct, but since I lacked space to make out a good case my bare assertions may have seemed weak and unsupported. Further, these statements did not agree with those of earlier scholars, nor with the popular view here in Iceland about the historical accuracy of the sagas; neither are they in line with the prevailing opinions of foreign scholars about the trustworthiness of oral traditions and the manner in which a saga-writer might have used such material. But it is quite profitless to wrangle about such intricate problems of scholarly investigation on the basis of loose speculations. All general statements about the Icelandic sagas must be regarded as so much hot air until those sagas which show themselves capable of being laid open to research are analysed one by one. Now *Hrafnkatla* is one of those sagas which, I believe, allow us to reach fairly definite conclusions on those points which are of most significance to the problem under discussion here. Therefore I will delay no longer in presenting my opinions.

First, I shall discuss the truthfulness of the saga wherever it can be tested against reasonably reliable sources. I have tried to work out this section in some detail because it is the basis of all that follows. Special stress is placed on the comparison of *Hrafnkatla* with earlier sources, but some reference is made to those methods of proof which, more recently, have been adduced to support a belief in the saga. Specific points are referred to which are less credible in themselves. I believe the reader will follow Chapter II better if he bears these points in mind:

1. When I have to compare *Hrafnkatla* with such sources as *Landnáma*, *Egla*, *Eyrbyggja*, &c., I have asked myself one question only: Have they recorded the particular incident more or less reliably than *Hrafnkatla*? Although on the whole I prefer them to *Hrafnkatla* whenever their authors have clearly had the opportunity to be better informed, I have been exclusively concerned in this section with their comparative validity as sources of information. I am not asserting in the process of this argument that these other sources in themselves are historically trustworthy.

2. I should like to warn those who trust implicitly in Icelandic traditions that such a trust is not vindicated by preferring a saga like *Hrafnkatla* to *Landnáma*, as has been done so often in the past. It sometimes looks as if scholars wished so strongly to believe in the individual sagas which were the objects of their special study that they did not consider the general implications of their theories about the sagas in general. There are firm grounds for believing that the main body of *Landnáma* was written early in the twelfth century, that the material was collected from the best available sourcemen, and that the authors had taken pains to record their material with precision and accuracy.[8] Naturally it may be objected that even then and with that method of approach it was impossible to leave a record which was truthful in every detail. Much had been forgotten in the interval between the Age of Settlement and the Age of

The Theme

Writing and there were insufficient sources to fill all the gaps. Now even though we grant that *Landnáma* is less accurate than a good contemporary source, we must still trust to it more than to the Icelandic sagas which were written up to 160 years later and which were recorded, to say the least, not only as historical sources but also for entertainment. By preferring the sagas as historical sources to *Landnáma* all possibility of a reasonable assessment of the old traditions was abandoned: the dead wood was allowed to stand while the green shoots were thrown into the fire.

Though I shall begin with an analysis of the historical accuracy of the saga, that is not my chief purpose. I am not an historian and it makes no difference to the history of Iceland whether *Hrafnkatla* is a reliable historical source or not. Here it is sufficient to say that if, in the past, it has been ransacked for information about our ancient customs and civilization, it should in the future be used more circumspectly.[9] The present observations on the subject-matter of *Hrafnkatla* are being made for quite a different purpose. If the saga, which cannot have been written down until 300 to 350 years after the events it recounts had been enacted, was reliable in its main features, then somehow it must have been preserved in a fixed form by oral tradition throughout the interval. Short and coherent as the saga was, it had a better chance of such preservation than many sagas one could name. Since no verses exist to verify its incidents, it might seem a particularly apposite example of the power of oral tradition to preserve a prose narrative accurately and for a long time. And if it had been written down at the time we have suggested, then there would be no limit to the notions we could advance about the growth and development of this oral art of preserving history. So, in the next place, we must examine the saga for irrefutable evidence of transcription from oral tradition and ask whether it was shaped gradually by a succession of story-tellers or composed by one man.

No intelligible answer can be given to this question unless some attention be paid to the artistic form in which this historical subject-matter is preserved. Does it resemble popular narrative art, or does it belong to a kind which it is easier to credit to a single author who was both a man of wide culture and a novelist?

Finally, from a wide variety of topics which demand further investigation I have omitted one of the most important, the collation of manuscripts. A fragment of the text is preserved on a vellum leaf which dates from the first half of the fifteenth century; otherwise the saga is extant only in late paper manuscripts which differ considerably from one another.[10] But although the saga has been so poorly preserved, it is generally agreed that there are no clear signs that it has been altered or recast in any of its main features. Therefore when the manuscripts are compared it is doubtful whether we have the right to regard anything which is found in all of them as later additions. Bearing all the manuscripts in mind, I have used the saga just as it is for my investigation and made no comment upon variant readings unless a particular point of interpretation is affected.[11]

II

HISTORICAL TRUTHFULNESS

THERE are many reasons why any attempt to consider the accuracy of *Hrafnkatla* as a record of real men and actual events should begin with the sons of Thjóstarr, Thorkell lepp and Thorgeirr. The saga cannot dispense with them. When they arrive on the scene there seems to be no hope for old Thorbjǫrn and Sámr. To them the power and reputation of Hrafnkell seems completely unassailable; on their own they are powerless against him, and all the chieftains have answered their request for help in the same way: none of them wished to risk his reputation by embarking on a quarrel with that same Hrafnkell godi[12] who had invariably imposed ignominious defeat on all who had opposed him. Then, by chance, they meet an adventurous hero, the proud Thorkell Thjóstarsson who has newly returned from Byzantium. At once he notices their wretchedness and is eager to make trial of his own prowess in some significant exploit. He persuades his brother Thorgeirr to back their plea and, because of their powerful aid and tenacity of purpose, Hrafnkell is defeated first at the Althing and later at his home (Aðalból). Without this there would have been no saga; the slaying of Einarr would have been one of those unatoned slayings by Hrafnkell which were not worth telling a story about. Moreover, since the brothers were not connected with the saga and were chieftains from quite a distant part of the country, we are entitled to hope that we should find sources of information about them more readily than about the other characters. Nowhere can the fidelity of the inherited traditions of the Austfirðir (which are thought to be present in this saga) be more thoroughly tested than in its account of these important men from the Vestfirðir.

The saga explains that these brothers are sons of a chieftain, Westfirthers by family and rearing, and that they share a godord[12] in Thorskafjǫrðr whose authority extends still wider in the Vestfirðir. It states further that their brother is Thormóðr from Garðar in Álptanes who had married Thórdís the daughter of Thórólfr Skalla-Grímsson from Borg. We shall examine these statements in detail.

Landnáma mentions Thormóðr Thjóstarsson a few times. His father is called Thjóstarr from Álptanes and his mother was Iðunn the daughter of Molda-Gnúpr. Nothing is said about Thjóstarr's family, but his marriage indicates that he must have been a man of some distinction even though he is not counted among the chieftains. Even in Álptanes his contemporaries, Ásbjǫrn Ǫssurarson, an original settler in Iceland, and Egill the son of Ásbjǫrn, must have been men of greater consequence than Thjóstarr. His son Thormóðr seems to have been an outstanding man who inherited the family characteristics of the Grindvíkings. When Thormóðr had newly returned from a voyage abroad, he proved that Ǫrn of Vælugerði had been slain 'un-outlawed' by shooting an arrow so far from his handbow that the place of Ǫrn's slaying fell within the bow-shot length.[13] In *Landnáma* his wife is called Thuríðr the daughter of Thorleifr, the son of Ávangr from Botn. Two of their children are also mentioned: Jórunn who was married to Red Illugi Hrólfsson from Innra-Hólm on Akranes and Bǫrkr who married Hallvǫr, a grand-daughter of Ketill gufa and Ýrr the daughter of Geirmundr heljarskinn. The son of Bǫrkr was Thórðr, the father of Auðunn from Brautarholt.[14]

Thus from what *Landnáma* says about Thormóðr, we may assert with confidence that the author of *Hrafnkatla* is inventing when he reports that the family of the sons of Thjóstarr are all Westfirthers. The whole family of Thormóðr—including his grandson Bǫrkr—had always lived to the south; significantly, though, Bǫrkr married a woman from the Vestfirðir.

Neither does it seem probable that Thormóðr could have been married to Thórdís the daughter of Thórólfr of Borg, since this is not mentioned in *Egla* or *Landnáma* and, as we stated above, *Landnáma* does not give the name of his wife. If, as must be assumed, the dispute at the Thing is supposed to

Historical Truthfulness

have taken place some years before the middle of the tenth century, then Thórdís (born about 935) would not have been of marrying age. It is fair to record that this is the one detail in the biographical study of the characters of *Hrafnkatla* which all scholars called in question, although Guðbrandur Vigfússon and Finnur Jónsson hazarded the guess that Thormóðr might have been Thórdís's first husband.[15]

Thorkell and Thorgeirr are nowhere mentioned except in *Hrafnkatla*. It is rather strange that, unlike Thormóðr, they should be overlooked by *Landnáma*, since, if we accept the saga's account of them, they must have been more important than he. 'Iðunn was the daughter of Molda-Gnúpr, and Thjóstarr of Álptanes married her. Thormóðr was their son.'[16] Why is there no mention of the godis in Thorskafjǫrðr? Now the events of quite a few sagas were set in the Vestfirðir and Breiðafjǫrðr in the tenth century. Knowing the temper of these brothers as it is displayed in *Hrafnkatla*, one would expect to come across them in the unfolding of events in these sagas. But they are not so much as mentioned by name and of no one is it said that he was descended from them. The amazing thing about these two western chieftains is that their memory has been preserved nowhere except in a saga from the other side of the country.

However, let us assume their existence. Let us assume first that the brothers were forgotten in the south because they had moved from the district, and that Thormóðr alone was remembered because his descendants continued to live there; secondly, that this was the only occasion on which they interfered in public affairs and that it satisfied them for life; and thirdly, that perhaps they both died young without leaving children. One question still remains unanswered: how did they ever attain to a position of authority in Thorskafjǫrðr?

Realizing all this, Guðbrandur Vigfússon set himself to solve the problem. It is common knowledge that Hallsteinn the son of Thórólfr Mostrarskegg was the first settler in Thorskafjǫrðr. *Landnáma* mentions only one son of his, Thorsteinn surtr, who settled down to the south of Breiðafjǫrðr.[17] But *Gull-Þóris saga,* the flimsiest of sources, names three of Hallsteinn's children, Thórarinn, Thuríðr, and Grímkell (who was illegitimate). It states that Thórarinn was slain; nothing is said about Grímkell, and thus only Thuríðr remains. Her existence gives Guðbrandur a way out, for he thinks it most likely that she became Thjóstarr's wife, and in this way the Thorskafjǫrðr godord was inherited by their sons. So the problem is neatly solved. There is only one drawback: as already stated, *Landnáma* says that Iðunn the daughter of Molda-Gnúpr was the wife of Thjóstarr. Of course he may have married twice, though this is nowhere mentioned. *Gull-Þóris saga*, the only authority for Thuríðr's existence, says that she was married to Ketilbjǫrn Gillason. Perhaps she might have married again when Ketilbjǫrn was killed! In this fashion one could obviously pile guess upon guess, but, then, the foundation should be more solid than *Gull-Þóris saga*, at least in the form in which we now know it.

Guðbrandur also deprived Hallsteinn of one son, Thorgils ǫrn, who is mentioned in *Eyrbyggja* and was the father of Thórðr, father of that Ragnhildr who married Thóroddr Thorbrandsson from Álptafjǫrðr. Although this is all we know about him, it is a doubtful procedure to deny him his patrimony because of a Thuríðr in *Gull-Þóris saga*. Further, we must not forget that Thorsteinn surtr (the only legitimate son of Hallsteinn mentioned in *Landnáma*) was still alive when the case between Sámr and Hrafnkell was disputed, and that he could have held the Thorskafjǫrðr godord even though he lived at Thórsnes. Again, although Hallsteinn is termed 'godi' in *Eyrbyggja*, there is some doubt surrounding this godord in the Vestfirðir. He could scarcely have wielded much authority since on the one side it was bounded by the Reyknesingar and on the other by Thorbjǫrn loki and Ketill gufa the son-in-law of Geirmundr heljarskinn. In *Hauksbók*'s list of the most distinguished settlers in the Western Quarter, Geirmundr, Úlfr skjálgi, and Thórðr Víkingsson are the three mentioned last, that is, farthest west. Hallsteinn is not mentioned. Nothing is more probable than that the three godords in the Thing-district

Historical Truthfulness

of Thorskafjǫrðr were held in *c.* 940 by Thórhall and Oddr, the sons of Ýrr, by Atli the Red, and by Thorkell from Alviðra. If, as *Gull-Þóris saga* says, Hallsteinn had a share in the temple of the Reyknesingar, then the authority which accompanied this share must have reverted to the Reyknesingar when the Althing was established since, by then, Hallsteinn was dead and his most influential son, Thorsteinn surtr, was living too far away to control thingmen to the north of Breiðafjǫrðr. Thorsteinn's non-residence in Thorskafjǫrðr strongly suggests that he had no authority to maintain in that district.

Whichever way we look at this question it is difficult to believe that the sons of Thjóstarr from Álptanes could have found any land to live on in Thorskafjǫrðr, and still more that subsequently they could have assumed authority there, while it is quite incredible that their power could have extended widely throughout the Vestfirðir. Such assumptions are as invalid as the statement made by Thorkell in the saga that they were the sons of a chieftain and, by birth and rearing, men of the Vestfirðir. Yet if all that *Hrafnkatla* says about them is wrong, and in view of the grave-like silence of all other sources, how can we avoid the conclusion that these brothers probably never existed? At least they could never have been chieftains anywhere, and all that the saga says about their power and consequent acts must be a complete fabrication.

To round off this argument I shall add that Guðbrandur, too, finally reached the conclusion that the sons of Thjóstarr had never existed; but, in his eyes, this made hardly any difference to the truthfulness of the saga. Instead of the 'three famous brothers from Thorskafjǫrðr', as he calls them, he calmly substitutes three other famous men from the Vestfirðir: Thorgrímr Thorsteinsson and Thorkell and Gísli, the sons of Súr. Hrafnkell's lawsuit probably never came before the Althing, only before Thingmúlathing. While sailing abroad these three men met bad weather, were driven into some fjord there in the east, and sauntered up to the Thing looking for amusement. There, with the support of the ship's crew, they carried the day.[18]

This is what Guðbrandur calls trying to 'get down to the rock-platform of fact'.

Yet despite this fantastic conjecture, Guðbrandur is surely right in stating that the lawsuit for the slaying of Einarr should not have gone straight to the Althing. Until the land was divided into Quarter districts it was the law of the land, as Ari says, 'that the lawsuit for a slaying should be prosecuted at the Thing which was nearest to the place of the slaying'.

One further question remains to be answered: Why is Thormóðr Thjóstarsson mentioned at all in the saga? He has nothing to do with its action and there is no suggestion that he assisted his brothers. Their support seems to have come entirely from the Vestfirðir *(vestan af landi)*. *Hrafnkatla* introduces few characters who are not necessary to the story but, in this instance, I believe the author has behaved like the too-clever burglar who leaves behind some trifle which eventually leads to his detection. By mentioning him in the saga the author seeks to express his thanks to Thormóðr for having lent him a name for the father of the brothers. In all probability he knew nothing about Thormóðr except what *Landnáma* says. The saga, to be sure, states that Thormóðr lived at Garðar. This is not recorded in any other source and it is the only statement about the sons of Thjóstarr in the saga which cannot be refuted by other evidence. But Garðar was a well-known farm in the thirteenth century and the author might well have added it on his own account. Was it perhaps Bǫrk's relationship by marriage with men of the Vestfirðir which gave the author the idea of endowing Bǫrk's uncles with this 'local habitation' in the west? Speculation on this point is valueless; some place of abode had to be found for them. Even so it can be stated with confidence that here there is no question of inherited oral tradition at work on its own account. Because Thormóðr played no part in the action he would have been dropped from any such oral tradition in the early stages. Can it be possible that tradition spoke of the sons of some other man called Thjóstarr and that our author, from his reading, made them into Thormóðr's brothers? This is not

Historical Truthfulness

very likely, especially when we recall that Thjóstarr from Álptanes is the only Icelander bearing that name in the old days.[19] No ordinary men could have played the role assigned to the brothers in the saga; such men must be sought among the chieftains—and there they are not to be found.

After this glimpse of the saga's treatment of two important subsidiary characters, it is proper that we should now turn to the principal character, Hrafnkell godi. Our first task is to show what other sources say about him.

Landnáma says this:

There was a man called Hrafnkell Hrafnsson who came to Iceland late in the period of settlement. He spent the first winter in Breiðdalr but in the spring he went up across the fell. He stopped in Skriðudalr and fell asleep there. Then he dreamed that a man came to him and told him to get up and move away as quickly as possible. He awoke and moved off. When he had gone but a short way the whole mountain-side collapsed and under it was a bear and a bull which he owned. Later Hrafnkell settled Hrafnkelsdalr and lived at Steinrøðarstaðir; his sons were Ásbjǫrn the father of Helgi and Thórir the father of Hrafnkell godi and grandfather of Sveinbjǫrn.

Following *Melabók*, *Þórðarbók* traces the descent of the family from Sveinbjǫrn down to Markús from Melar.

Hrafnkell godi is included in the list of the most distinguished settlers in the Eastern Quarter and among the greatest chieftains in the land 'at the time when the country had been inhabited for sixty years'.[20]

Njála says that about 1010 A.D. Hrafnkelsstaðir was inhabited by Hrafnkell, son of Thórir, who was the son of Hrafnkell Hrafnsson (in other manuscripts Hrafnkell is called *raumr* or the son of Runólfr). Thórir the son of Hrafnkell the Younger (cf. *Landnáma*) is named there, but no mention is made of Sveinbjǫrn. *Njála* is a noteworthy source here since it follows no known version of *Landnáma*.

Droplaugarsona saga says a great deal about the descendants of Hrafnkell; namely, that at the end of the tenth century Helgi the son of Ásbjǫrn lived first at Oddsstaðir (above Hafrsá) and later at Mjóvanes, while Hrafnkell the son of Thórir lived at Hafrsá. It also mentions a contemporary farmer named Thorgeirr, apparently quite unrelated to them, who was living at Hrafnkelsstaðir.

Brandkrossa Þáttr follows *Landnáma* in everything it says about Hrafnkell. It adds that Thórir lived at Steinrøðarstaðir after his father's day, that Ásbjǫrn settled the farm at Lokhellur —which is now called Hrafnkelsstaðir—and that Helgi the son of Ásbjǫrn sold this farm to Hrafnkell Thórisson and afterwards inhabited Oddstaðir himself. If we accept this account, then Hrafnkelsstaðir was named after Hrafnkell the Younger. Although *Brandkrossa Þáttr* is not a very reliable source, it is worth noting that its author either did not know *Hrafnkatla* at all or any traditions similar to its record, or else he ignored them and preferred to follow *Landnáma*.

Before I proceed further with a comparison of these sources and *Hrafnkatla*, I must touch on two points in it which are indirectly paralleled in *Landnáma*.

According to the saga, Hrafnkell is the son of Hallfreðr who came to Iceland by ship to Breiðdalr and finally settled down at Hallfreðarstaðir in Tunga; according to *Landnáma*, Thórðr Thórólfsson hálmi settled the lands at Tunga. Thus Hallfreðr could not have been an independent settler. Yet his son settled land for himself and is later included in *Landnáma* among the most distinguished settlers in the Quarter and the most powerful chieftains in the country at the end of the Age of Settlement. On any showing this is a strange and incredible story.

After Hrafnkell was driven from Aðalból he bought land on credit at Lokhilla and quickly became the leading man in the district. Now the saga itself says that at that particular time 'the greatest number of ships had come from Norway to Iceland; men then settled most of the land in that district in Hrafnkell's day'. Now this was supposed to have happened towards the middle of the tenth century and, however strongly people believe in the rest of the saga, they all agree that this particular

Historical Truthfulness

statement is absurd. How then, in a few years, did Hrafnkell rise to such power in this new district? Even if we allow him exceptional gifts, such advancement would be conceivable only if there had been no other important men in this area. *Landnáma* says that Brynjólfr the Old, the son of Thorgeirr Vestarsson, settled 'all the district of Fljótsdalr above Hengiforsá to the west and above Gilsá to the east, and all of Skriðudalr together with the land as far as Eyvindará. He acquired a great deal of the original settlement of Uni Garðarsson and settled there his relatives and kinsmen by marriage.' *Landnáma* gives Brynjólfr thirteen children. To his brother Ævarr he allotted all of Skriðudalr above Gilsá but to Ásrǫðr, who had married his stepdaughter and niece, he gave all the land between Gilsá and Eyvindará. Kolskeggr *fróði* traced his descent from Ásrǫðr. This was a powerful family group. Brynjólfr is included in the list of distinguished settlers in the Eastern Quarter, and his descendants seem to have been godis in succession: Ǫzurr, Bersi, and Hólmsteinn, who is involved in events both in *Droplaugarsona saga* and in *Njála*.

Penniless and defeated as he was Hrafnkell must be supposed to have settled down in the heart of the original settlement of Brynjólfr the Old and, in a few years, to have become the sole arbiter of it all. This simply cannot be true. There is no more room for the power of Hrafnkell in Fljótsdalr than there was for that of the sons of Thjóstarr in Thorskafjǫrðr.[21]

There is the further point that *Droplaugarsona saga* (which is earlier and more clearly dependent on oral tradition than *Hrafnkatla*) states, as was mentioned above, that two of Hrafnkell's grandsons, Helgi Ásbjarnarson and Hrafnkell Thórisson, both lived in this district in later times. Now both were related to Brynjólfr the Old's family—Helgi marrying Droplaug the daughter of Bersi, and Hólmsteinn the son of Bersi marrying Áslaug the sister of Hrafnkell Thórisson. These cousins shared a godord and it may well have been this inherited godord (down from Jǫkulsdalr) which they enlarged with new thingmen from Fljótsdalr and Hérað. It is not unlikely that, because he knew something about these descendants of Hrafnkell, the author of the saga conceived the idea of making their authority east of the heath a survival from earlier times.

Possibly the author of *Hrafnkatla* knew *Droplaugarsona saga*. His reference to Sighvatr and Snorri, the sons of Hallsteinn from Víðivellir, suggests it. *Droplaugarsona saga* also talks about the sons of Hallsteinn, namely Thórðr, Thorkell, and Eindriði. When Jakob Jakobsen stated in his introduction to *Austfirðinga sǫgur* that these are the same men but that it was doubtful which saga gave the names correctly, he completely ignored the question of chronology. The sons of Hallsteinn in *Hrafnkatla* were fully grown men in the middle of the tenth century, while those in *Droplaugarsona saga* were not only still alive *c.* 1000 but their father was just then getting married for the second time. Then why not be bold and assume that Hallsteinn in *Droplaugarsona saga* is the son of either Sighvatr or Snorri? Unfortunately the saga itself states that this Hallsteinn from Víðivellir was called 'the Broad-daler', so that he could not have had his home in Fljótsdalr. The essential difference is that in *Hrafnkatla* the sons of Hallsteinn are nothing more than names, mere undistinguished supporters of Hrafnkell, while in *Droplaugarsona saga* the slaying of Hallsteinn from Víðivellir, second husband of Droplaug, is essential to the main story. One could of course believe in the remarkable coincidence that within a span of about fifty years *two* Hallsteinns, quite unrelated to each other, had lived at Víðivellir, but it is surely easier to assume that the author of *Hrafnkatla* recalled the sons of Hallsteinn in *Droplaugarsona saga* and inserted them into his own saga in order to show that he was not completely ignorant of the names of Hrafnkell's supporters. He was aware of the chronological discrepancies and so gave them different names.[22] On the other hand, it is hardly likely that he had any source for 'the sons of Hrólfr from Hrólfsstaðir', other than the name of the farm.[23] For the other important characters in *Hrafnkatla* there are no sources available for comparison. The saga names a wife of Hrafnkell who is not mentioned in *Landnáma*, Oddbjǫrg the

Historical Truthfulness

daughter of Skjǫldólfr from Laxárdalr. *Landnáma* offers two Skjǫldólfrs, both from the Eastern Quarter, but there is no Laxárdalr there. Nor is it likely that this name was preserved orally, since Oddbjǫrg has little to do with the story and her family nothing at all.

The treatment of place-names of *Hrafnkatla*, it has been argued, demands that its claim to historical truth should be preferred to that of *Landnáma*. The author was deeply interested in their derivations and scattered a great number throughout the saga. It is quite true that sagas have preserved many place-names and that place-names may have helped to preserve traditions. But, in addition, it is well to remember that place-names themselves can occasion the composition of sagas, folk-tales, and romances which seek to explain their origin. Indeed, place-names have often been located or derived indiscriminately by misunderstanding what the sagas say. Examples of such fictitious derivations are well known. In the *tún* at Hǫll in Thveráhlíðr is displayed the tomb of Halla, a settler's wife;[24] Hítardalr gives rise to the saga about Hít the troll-wife; Ármannsfell to *Ármannssaga*; Hvalfjǫrður and Hvalvatn to the tales about Rauðhǫfði; similarly there is the story about Esja in *Kjalnesinga saga*, &c., &c. In the Family Sagas, and even in *Landnáma*, there are undoubtedly many more stories than we now suspect which were invented merely to explain the origin of place-names. Some examples of place-names which have been located erroneously include Lǫgberg (Spǫngina) in Thingvellir, Dritsker near Haugsnes,[25] and Gunnarshaugr near Hlíðarendi. Many place-names have even been derived from folk-tales, one of them being Bárðarlaug in Snæfellsnes.

If the first chapter of *Hrafnkatla* be compared with *Landnáma*, many differences will indeed be found between them, but still there remains enough common ground to suggest that the saga writer could easily have had *Landnáma* before him as he wrote or else that he had read it and remembered it. The principal difference is that while *Landnáma* describes the journeys of Hrafnkell Hrafnsson, the saga describes those of Hallfreðr the father of

Hrafnkell. The stopping-places on the journey are the same. *Landnáma* says that Hrafnkell spent the first winter in Breiðdalr; the saga says that Hallfreðr had spent the first winter in Breiðdalr and set up house there. 'During the winter a foreign serving-woman called Arnthrúðr died there and this place has therefore since been called Arnthrúðarstaðir.' The name of this farm cannot be found in any other source, early or late. The name Arnthrúðr is rare, but it is a Norse and not a foreign name. Whether the farm had been unnamed until this woman died or whether it was then the custom to celebrate the death of servants by naming farms after them I do not know, but if at any time there was a farm named Arnthrúðarstaðir in Breiðdalr, it seems not improbable that this derivation at least was an invention of the author. The next move in the journey is to Skriðudalr. Here the difference is that Hrafnkell rested to eat food whereas Hallfreðr builds a house—though the narrative goes on to state that the house was built in Geitdalr, one of the two branches of Skriðudalr. Both sources agree that a man appeared in a dream to H(-rafnkell, -allfreðr), warning him against staying there any longer, and that afterwards a landslide descended on the resting place (or house) and destroyed two animals—a boar and a bull in *Landnáma*, a boar and a goat in *Hrafnkatla*. (The text is not very reliable, but it is probably best to agree with Jakobsen that the original reading is more likely to have been *gǫltur* than *geit*, *gulgeit*, or *gaulbert*.[26]) The name Geitdalr resembles a host of other place-names which are derived from the circumstance that certain animals had grazed near a certain spot, but there may well be another explanation in this case. On the other hand, it is certain that though there have been numerous landslides in many parts of Skriðudalr, as the name indicates, the biggest and best known occurred in Geitdalr. In the *Prestssaga* of Gudmundr the Good (cf. *Konungsannáll* and *Flateyarannáll*) it is recorded that in 1185 'a landslide occurred in Geitdalr in the east and killed 18 men'. The remains of this great landslide, which men of later times probably connected with the *Landnáma* narrative, may have given the author

Historical Truthfulness

of *Hrafnkatla* an idea for the precise location of Hallfreðr's home, and thus caused the substitution of a goat for a bull.

If we now prefer to trust *Landnáma* and the genealogy in *Njála*, thus accepting that Hrafnkell was the son of Hrafn and not of Hallfreðr, then the saga's explanation of Hallfreðargata (leading from Hallfreðarstaðir up into Hrafnkelsdalr) must become yet another of its fictitious place-name derivations.[27] Why did Hallfreðargata extend from Hallfreðarstaðir to Hrafnkelsdalr? What errand had any Hallfreðr along this road? It may have been the name of this path which gave the author the idea of making Hrafnkell the son of Hallfreðr.

We ought to approach the name of Eyvindr Bjarnason in a similar spirit of scepticism. If the sons of Þjóstarr never existed, if Hrafnkell was never forced down into Fljótsdalr, if these are fictions, then it is obvious that Eyvindr and his slaying are equally fictitious. He bears reasonably clear marks of artifice. Not only has he, like Þorkell lepp, spent some time at Byzantium at a period when it is doubtful whether any Varangians had arrived there, but he is attended by a page in the manner of a foreign chieftain. The place-names Eyvindarfjǫll and Eyvindardalr existed and the author extracted from them a name for his character and thus gained confirmation for his story in later generations. Eyvindardalr runs east out of Jǫkulsdalr, along it flows Eyvindará, and Eyvindarfjǫll is somewhat inland from the road which leads from Fljótsdalr to Aðalból. Even assuming that someone called Eyvindr had been slain up there on the heath, it is difficult to believe that all these places were named after him. Probably the name was first used in Jǫkulsdalr to describe Eyvindardalr and Eyvindará and later transferred to the heath. But what of *Eyvindartorfa*?[28] The name is now unknown, but if such a name had existed it is likely that, like other names discussed below, the place was named from the saga and not the other way round. Perhaps the author, who certainly knew the district, had seen a *torfa* suitable for the site of a battle. Incidentally, this mound has a very remarkable history which does not bear directly on the veracity of *Hrafnkatla* but throws light on the fallible judgement of men in the nineteenth century. When Sigurður Vigfússon toured the eastern part of Iceland in 1890 he searched for the *torfa* without success. He says: '*Eyvindartorfa* had been situated where one leaves the bog and goes up into the fell, but it has now been completely scattered by the wind and no trace left. However, Sigfúss from Skjǫgrastaðir, a sound man and learned in old names, tells me that his father had seen *Eyvindartorfa* with a barrow on it, but even then the greensward had been so eroded that nothing remained but a small fringe around the barrow.'[29] This *torfa* certainly behaved in a most reprehensible manner. This is how it is described in *Hrafnkatla*: 'A *torfa* overgrown with lyme-grass and very much eroded by the wind; its banks stood high above the surrounding area.' If the *torfa* had served as any kind of defended place for five men, it could not have been very large. It is immaterial whether the saga's description refers to its condition in the tenth or the thirteenth century. The *torfa* seems to have withstood the assaults of wind and sandstorm for six to eight centuries. Then suddenly the whim takes it to disintegrate just before the first archaeologist arrives to investigate it. At least Sigurður ought then to have made a search for the bones of Eyvindr and his fellows (which had been in the barrow) since they should have been lying about on the site of the *torfa*, and ought still to be there.[30]

Among the incorrect interpretations of place-names in the saga should be included the name of Hrafnkelsstaðir, since it is quite unlikely that the elder Hrafnkell had at any time moved down into Fljótsdalr. Without our placing absolute trust in *Brandkrossa Þáttr*, its explanation that the farm was named after Hrafnkell Thórisson seems likely to be much nearer the truth (cf. *Njála*).

We must now turn our attention to that other abode of Hrafnkell which is called Steinrøðarstaðir in *Landnáma* and Aðalból [Manor House] in the saga. Possibly Aðalból was inhabited in the thirteenth century, even though it is not mentioned in any other source.[31] The nearest we get to it is a mention of another farm in the dale which was inhabited at a later date. Nothing is known about Steinrøðarstaðir itself except what *Landnáma* says, and on this point all scholars seem to prefer and trust the saga's statement. Does not the very name 'Aðalból' suggest the residence of the most powerful man in the dale? This alone would explain the author's deviation from *Landnáma*, particularly if, when he was writing, Steinrøðarstaðir had been abandoned and Aðalból was still inhabited. For it is extremely unlikely that the source for *Landnáma* had deliberately invented a substitute for Aðalból and, at that, a name which could not be explained. If it were a question here of two conjectures and I might be permitted to borrow an idiom from the comparison of variant manuscript readings, I would call Aðalból *lectio facilior* and Steinrøðarstaðir *lectio difficilior*; the latter belonging to that kind of information which can be accepted because it is unlikely to be a fiction.

For the better understanding of this and other matters in the saga, a brief account of the habitation of Hrafnkelsdalr will be of some value. The saga does not give the number of farms in the dale, but we are left to assume that there were many. *Brandkrossa Þáttr* states that there had been nearly twenty farms and other traditions refer to fourteen. Like the number of inhabitants of Ǫrnólfsdalr given in *Hænsa-Þóris saga* this is obviously an exaggeration. *Hrafnkatla* mentions four farms in the dale—Aðalból, Hóll, Leikskálar, and Laugarhús; there were probably a few more in the Age of Settlement. Apart from *Landnáma*, *Hrafnkatla*, and *Brandkrossa Þáttr*, there are no early sources for the settling of the dale. It is said that it was laid waste during the Black Death, but in Iceland there is an epidemic of such explanations of abandoned areas. Bishop Vilchin's inventory of the church at Valthjófsstaðir for the year 1397 mentions the 'summer-pasture land of Laugarhús' which is one of the most desirable places in the dale.[32] Our knowledge of the dale since the middle of the sixteenth century suggests that dwellings there were few and of uncertain duration.[33] So that if I had to guess how the valley was settled in the earliest days, I should offer this as the likeliest pattern: Hrafnkelsdalr was settled by a man who had newly arrived from Norway and judged the land by its inviting summer appearance. There are many such instances of land which the first settlers thought cultivable but which speedily disappointed their first hopes and was allowed to go waste: for example, Langavatnsdalr, Geitland, and Thórsmǫrk. Its later history shows that Hrafnkelsdalr was a really inhospitable district when it was put to trial: it is about 1,000 feet above sea-level, the winter there must have been severe, grazing lands soon deteriorated through the constant cropping of straying cattle and through tree-felling, and the land began to suffer from wind-erosion. It can be said to be less likely (following the saga) that Hrafnkell settled the dale after he had been in Iceland some years than that (as *Landnáma* states) he settled there after his first winter.

We may accept the view that towards the end of the tenth century the size of the settlement in the dale had begun to shrink. This is best shown by the fact that both of Hrafnkell's grandsons had found establishments for themselves below the heath. There are more or less trustworthy accounts of very bad seasons around 975—the first exceedingly severe winter in Iceland—and it is possible that Hrafnkelsdalr never recovered after this date. Further, there were plenty of hard seasons in the eleventh and twelfth centuries which would have severely hampered a full settlement: for example, the volcanic eruption of Trǫlladyngjur in 1151. If Hrafnkelsdalr had already been reduced to waste when the saga was composed, it would be easier to understand why the author had never been there and why he was emboldened to name places after his own fancy and conjecture.

Returning to our earlier statement that *Landnáma* (the evidence of the wisest men of the twelfth century) gives a more trustworthy account of the name of the dwelling of Hrafnkell goði than *Hrafnkatla*, we still have to consider the relationship between Steinrøðarstaðir and Aðalból. Most people agree that at Aðalból is one of the most attractive building-sites in the dale, even though Sigurður Vigfússon preferred the view from the

Historical Truthfulness

spot where he thought that Laugarhús ought to have been situated. Assuming that Hrafnkell had lived at Aðalból, Sigurður found there the site of his outhouses and hall; he even hunted around for Hrafnkell's barrow, dug it up, and carried off the bones to Reykjavík.[34]

One small matter, however, caused him a great deal of trouble. Below the farm at Aðalból, where Freyfaxi's Bluff [*Freyfaxahamarr*] ought to have stood with a deep pool beneath, there are only level fields. But this intrepid searcher was not dismayed. There are few dales in Iceland which do not boast some kind of rocky outcrop, if one looks hard enough. Sigurður found Freyfaxi's Bluff—'as it is still called to this day'—admittedly 5–6 kilometres from Aðalból and in a ravine with not even the smallest trickle of a stream. But to make up for this slight defect he found the site of an old sheep-cote just below the bluff:[35] obviously this must have been Hrafnkell's temple! Now all was clear; the text of the saga must have been altered a little in the manuscripts, but the author was absolved from all error and the saga's truth vindicated.

The saga's explanation of Hrossageilar suggests that the author, believing Aðalból to have always been situated where it now stands, had viewed the site of the house and the path from the heath (see below) but had not gone up to the farm; thus he had allowed himself to guess at the presence of a non-existent bluff. We are therefore faced with these alternatives. Either, as we have already suggested, an Aðalból, inhabited or deserted, existed in the thirteenth century in the same place as it is now (which may have been the site of Steinrøðarstaðir) and the author selected it for Hrafnkell's farm, or the author himself had given this name to Hrafnkell's house instead of the original Steinrøðarstaðir and thereafter the new name from the saga was adopted when the present farm was set up there late in the eighteenth century. This must remain an open question unless other as yet unknown sources bring fresh light to bear on the problem.

I shall not take the study of place-names in *Hrafnkatla* any farther because I wish to leave this to those with better qualifications, and because it has little to do with the truthfulness of the saga. If an author believes that a story was enacted in a certain district, it is not surprising if he describes accurately what he has seen and examined. And even though the authors of our ancient stories had no first-hand knowledge of local conditions, it was far easier for them to discover factual information about static things which had remained unaltered than to obtain accurate accounts of long-past events. An author's knowledge of places can never be a firm foundation for the truthfulness of any narrative, but his negligence as to their correct interpretation (even when they are places very near to his native heath) may throw some light on the degree to which he was concerned to be accurate.

Generally the interpretation of place-names has been confused with the question of historical veracity. The Icelandic people, steeped in the sagas, who have in later ages renamed many places after the sagas, have not made the scholar's task of identification any easier. One can, however, make a shrewd guess as to the chance which the place-names of Hrafnkelsdalr had of remaining unaltered and free from the influence of the saga during all those centuries when the dale was completely (or practically) uninhabited.[36]

Hrafnkell's title, *Freysgoði* [Priest of Frey], for which *Hrafnkatla* is the sole authority, plays a significant and dramatic part in the saga. It is highly suspicious that neither *Landnáma* nor *Njála* appends this title to Hrafnkell's name. In the Family Sagas only two other chieftains carry this title: one is Thorgrímr Thorsteinsson who is named so once in the later version of *Gísla saga* (though the other version mentions Frey-worship), and the other is Þórðr Ǫzurarson who is so designated in many places and whose descendants were called *Freysgyðlingar* [Frey worshippers]. According to the experts, only three place-names in Iceland are directly connected with the name of Frey: Freysnes in Ǫræfi and Freyshólar and Freysnes by Lagarfljót. Now

Freyshólar is an outlying farm of that Hafrsá where Hrafnkell Thórisson is said to have lived, and Freysnes is quite near to it and to Mjóvanes, the home of Helgi Ásbjarnarson. Possibly there is a suggestion here that some of Hrafnkell's descendants[37] may have worshipped Frey, and this is a fact worth noting, but what we can make of this depends to a large extent on the age of these place-names and the date at which Hrafnkell's kinsmen moved into this district. One thing is certain: if Frey-worship had persisted in Hrafnkell's family until the conversion of Iceland to Christianity, then everything that the saga says about Hrafnkell having derived all his misfortune from Freyfaxi and about his subsequent refusal to sacrifice and believe in the gods is mere invention.[38] But it is scarcely worth while calling attention to this.

Though the saga is generally realistic in tone, some incidents, uncorroborated by other sources, are clearly unbelievable. For example, Einarr Thorbjarnarson wished to catch the horses 'and they were now shy which were never accustomed to be ridden by men, except for Freyfaxi who was as still as if he had been rooted to the spot'. This is very effective and shows that here the Fates are at work; it excuses Einarr and makes his death inevitable. Of Freyfaxi's behaviour after Einarr had loosed him I shall only say that similar tales of riding-horses are extant,[39] and the author may well be drawing here from life. Equally effective is the description of the pride of old Thorbjǫrn when he refuses to accept the generous offers of Hrafnkell unless arbitrators should be appointed between them. The needs of artistic unity demand this in order to set the story in motion and to place a favourable construction on Hrafnkell's attitude to Einarr's death so that his final return to power is justified. But this is an unusual saga since its actors are men of such unequal stations in life. Again the description in the saga of Thjóstarr's sons' treatment of the temple is quite absurd. It recalls Hrappr in *Njála* or Búi in *Kjalnesinga*, and if we are looking for historical accuracy this is unhappy company. Surely, if Sámr was to maintain the temple and the sacrifice—as was only right and proper—this burning was to his disadvantage. The episode, it is generally agreed, is an embroidery on the story due to the zeal of a Christian author, possibly a cleric. The whole story of Hrafnkell's new prosperity at Hrafnkelsstaðir is equally incredible; even if we ignore the neighbours among whom this took place (see above), it is hard to accept that this new wealth and power were acquired in only six years.[40] For one rare moment the author has lost his sure touch and shows no discretion, since it is quite conceivable that Hrafnkell could have taken revenge on a much more powerful opponent than Sámr without having to be puffed out into a mighty chieftain. Indisputably, though, as will be shown later, this lack of discretion reveals another side of Hrafnkell's character. We have already referred to the two Varangians, Thorkell lepp and Eyvindr; they provide a second instance of undue extravagance. The third is the torture which Hrafnkell and his men have to endure—and this will be discussed more fully later. Other examples could be adduced of events which have the flavour of fiction rather than of sober fact, but they can best be discussed when we consider the author's treatment of his subject-matter.

By now it is quite clear that very few incidents in *Hrafnkatla* have the support of other sources, in fact only those where the saga and *Landnáma* agree: that Hrafnkell had been a chieftain who settled in Hrafnkelsdalr and lived there and had two sons, Ásbjǫrn and Thórir. Much of the rest of the saga must be regarded as fictitious—and this includes the main events. Some things in the story, like the title 'Freysgoði' (though that too is open to doubt) must be left undecided, and yet others will be discussed below. Where, then, did the saga writer obtain the material for those events in his story which are without foundation in history? Are they inventions of the writer of the story (the author, as we have occasionally termed him already for the sake of brevity) or was the material actually shaped by those people who entertained their countrymen with their skill in the art of telling stories? To answer such questions we must first consider what is known about the saga's sources.

III

SOURCES

THE clearest indication of the use of written sources in the composition of *Hrafnkatla* is the genealogical tree of Haraldr hárfagri with which the saga opens: it conforms to a similar tree at the beginning of *Íslendingabók*. The manuscripts give no shadow of support for the assumption that this table is a later addition as Finnur Jónsson wished to regard it. The tree need not have been copied directly from *Íslendingabók*, it could have been obtained from any other book based on it; how it came into the saga-writer's hands is of little importance.

It has already been suggested that the author knew *Droplaugarsona saga*; this is almost a self-evident assumption since that saga[41] was written in the same district and must have been older than *Hrafnkatla*. What he takes from it is unimportant [i.e. the sons of Hallsteinn] and no attempt is made to link the two sagas together; for example, Hrafnkell's grandsons, who figure in *Droplaugarsona saga*, are not mentioned in our saga. It is more important for our purpose to understand the relationship between *Hrafnkatla* and *Landnáma*. Because there is considerable divergence between their narratives it has always been assumed that they were unconnected. On thing is obvious: if the author knew *Landnáma* thoroughly and was especially anxious to follow earlier scholarship as closely as possible, then he must have known that his saga conflicted both directly and indirectly with *Landnáma*. Conversely, if the author's primary purpose was to compose a work of fiction, then he would take from *Landnáma* only those things which were necessary to set the story in motion, and even those he would adapt to his own purposes.

The name of Thormóðr Thjóstarsson was most probably taken from *Landnáma* because it is mentioned in no other source older than *Hrafnkatla*, and it is unlikely that his name would have been preserved orally in the Austfirðir.

Landnáma and the first chapters of the saga disagree on many points of detail, but the general outline of events is the same in both: (1) a winter stay in Breiðdalr; (2) a resting-place in Skriðudalr, a warning dream, a landslide descending on the resting-place immediately after departure with the destruction of animals beneath it; (3) the settling of land to the west of Lagarfljót. As was suggested above, these discrepancies could have been due to the deliberate alterations of an author. This is more likely than the alternative explanation, that the Hrafnkell tradition had been corrupted in the east after *Landnáma* was written and that the author of the saga was unaware of it. The education of the man who decided to write the story of Hrafnkell godi must have been curiously circumscribed if he was able to obtain the family tree of Haraldr hárfagri, the name of Thormóðr Thjóstarsson, and the sons of Hallsteinn from written sources and yet remain ignorant of what *Landnáma* had written about his saga-hero. Those who study without prejudice the handling of the subject-matter in *Hrafnkatla* should be able to agree that the saga is unlikely to be the work of an unlearned man. On the contrary, I think it more probable that the author had read a greater part of the literature of Iceland that was extant in his day though he used but a tithe of his knowledge in the composition of this one short saga. Still, such an education must have helped him to form a just estimate of the best field for the exercise of his own powers and supported him in his determination to shape his own style.

The saga betrays little awareness of foreign literature (in translation), but the author may well have known something of it. His is a saga about men. Only three women are mentioned by name, Arnthrúðr (a female slave), Oddbjǫrg Skjǫldólfsdóttir, and Thórdís Thórólfsdóttir, and these are mere names. Hrafnkell's own anonymous serving-woman has much more to do with the story. Her ranting is finely portrayed when she lets her tongue wag furiously and she says many things which are only too true, though her intentions are evil. Even she is not an independent creation, since she is used by the author merely to add one more sidelight to the development of Hrafnkell's character. Hrafnkell is indolent and slow to act; he needs goading and would not have permitted such freedom of speech to any of his housecarles or his neighbours; he cannot become angry with a servant-maid, particularly one who gives expression to his secret thoughts.

Because women play such a small part in the saga it is not to be expected that it should show any influence of the foreign sagas of chivalry with their portrayal of love. For all that, the author may have read them without allowing them to influence him. On the whole *Hrafnkatla* is an unromantic saga. In particular, Hrafnkell and Thorgeirr, the two strongest-minded characters, are hard-headed men with no chivalrous notions to stand in their way. Even so, isolated touches reveal traces of another way of thinking. Thorkell lepp and Eyvindr Bjarnason have been in search of fame all the way to Byzantium; Thorkell is dressed in a leaf-green kirtle with an ornamented sword in his hand, and Eyvindr rides with a handsome shield which gleams in the sun. Such highly-coloured descriptive touches, however, are sparingly used. Hrafnkell rides to the shieling in blue clothes with only his axe as a weapon, and when he sets out after Eyvindr his men arm themselves 'for business' (and not for display). It is a touch of bombast to allow Eyvindr a *skósveinn* [a page] after the fashion of foreign noblemen, for there is no other mention of this kind of servant among Icelanders in the older sagas.

The torture which Hrafnkell and his men undergo seems to have an un-Icelandic flavour. Here I think we can be confident that we have to deal with foreign subject-matter, although it is open to dispute whether it was obtained from oral tales or from books. It may be mentioned that in Saxo's narrative, on one occasion, Jarmericus punished the Wends by hanging forty of them with a wolf between each pair, and on another occasion by ordering ropes to be drawn through the pierced hams of some of their chieftains and allowing bulls to tear them to pieces.[42] Possibly, the earlier source which was used by Saxo and the saga is still in existence somewhere.

Those written sources which were used directly throw a very faint light on the sources of the subject-matter of the saga. We must now consider whether it was derived from tradition or oral tales. At this stage in the argument I shall make but a few observations on this topic.

The saga makes no mention of traditions or different versions of traditions about the same incident; not once, not even in deference to custom, does it employ the phrase 'it is said'. The author speaks as one with authority and never seems to have any doubts as to what happened and when.

When men have thought that they were able to corroborate incidents in the old sagas which are not taken from verses they have understandably assumed the presence of old, inherited traditions. Examples of this nature are admittedly not plentiful and some of them are not well supported by other evidence; but this is too big a subject to be debated here. Is it then possible to conclude that the chances of the subject-matter of a saga being based on oral tradition are in inverse proportion to its unreliability? This need not necessarily be the case: popular lore is capable of much distortion, even of being mostly fictitious in origin (cf. the *Fornaldarsǫgur*). Perhaps our mistrust of the honesty of the East Icelandic story-tellers will go too far if we charge them with having invented those main incidents in the saga which, as we have seen, can never have taken place. Such a mistrust scarcely accords with investigations of the Norwegian and Icelandic stories of later times which contain, admittedly, lapses of memory and misrepresentations, embroideries and falsehoods in plenty, but which usually retain in their main incidents a core of historical truth. Yet it would be rash to discount such a possibility in advance. Someone must have composed what is invented, so why could it not be the man who told the story for entertainment as much as the man who wrote it down? Even if this view were examined to the exclusion of all other considerations, the evidence is weighted heavily in favour of a saga-writer, principally for two reasons. First, his handling of the subject-matter, wherever it came from, shows clearly that he was a wise man. If he had been retelling a story or tradition which he believed to be mainly true, his judgement would have been more alert and he would have taken some precautions against error; at least he would have had some faint inkling that the story was told differently in *Landnáma*. His very lack of hesitation in telling the story suggests that he was not concerned with historical truth. Such an attitude belongs more naturally to an author drawing solely on his own invention than to a chronicler of facts. Second, it is more credible that influences from written sources—even though they should be no more than those we have indicated—should have come directly from written sagas rather than from oral sourcemen acting as links between such written sources and the saga-writer. In one place, the genealogies from *Íslendingabók*, this is quite certainly the case.

Although it will always be difficult to draw a distinct line between those parts of the subject-matter of sagas which are derived from oral tradition and those which are due to the alterations, additions, and fictions of the authors, one can often make a good guess from the nature of the material and the author's treatment of it. The popular tale has one easily recognizable feature: the original account has split into different versions so that a scrupulous saga-writer sometimes mentions that a particular incident is not always told in the same way or else he slips up and tells us the same tale twice in different versions. An example of both these things happening is found in *Reykdæla saga*. Another recognizable feature is the tendency of popular oral tradition to attract to itself material from current tales and folk-lore. Nor is it at all accurate to maintain that those tales are more faithful recordings of oral stories which are presented with a more realistic tone. In fact it is probably nearer the truth to say that the author of *Eyrbyggja* had access to more popular material about the Fróðá-hauntings and the ghost of Thórólfr Clubfoot than he had about the interchanges between Snorri and Arnkell godi. Many incidents in the sagas are of such a nature that it is hard to believe that any writer of fiction took pleasure in composing them or could have assumed that any reader would have been amused by them; such incidents never deal with the main story and only serve to complicate the main course of events. Frequently the authors of sagas are unable to find the appropriate places for such things in the narrative and this can lead to strange irresolution in their treatment. The scrupulous zeal of the antiquary with his desire to save everything from oblivion has to struggle with the taste and endowment of the artist. Such sagas become heterogeneous, like *Bjarnar saga Hítdælakappa*, which goes to pieces in the middle because a scholar's prejudice allows gossip from the district and digressions inconsistent with the main action to remain in the saga. Similarly in *Gunnlaugs saga*, with a large element of fiction in its composition, one notices that the author cannot control his material (cf. some of the verses of Gunnlaugr with the trivial incidents which are introduced in order to explain them).

When the construction of *Hrafnkatla* is analysed from this point of view it becomes clear that it has little kinship with popular traditions. In it there are no references to discrepant traditions and no popular superstitions, since neither the dream of Hallfreðr (taken from *Landnáma*) nor the belief in destiny, which is present in all the older sagas, can be so described. The few things in the saga which might betray the antiquarian and are manifestly unnecessary for the main story (such as the genealogy at the beginning, the statement about Thormóðr Thjóstarsson, and the legal explanations) are all of a kind which could scarcely have been derived from oral tradition. Some are clearly from books; some (many of the explanations of place-names, for instance) have long been regarded as evidence of an author's hand. The scholarly influence was so strong in the Icelandic historical writings that even the best writers of fictitious sagas felt it more seemly to display their erudition as, in fact, the genealogies and the legal knowledge in *Njála* show quite plainly. Only one thing in our saga puzzles the reader: 'the good spear' of Hrafnkell which is mentioned at the end of the saga. This is

Sources

obviously the same spear that Hrafnkell took with him from Aðalból and one feels that it ought have been described previously at greater length or that it should have been mentioned when previous killings are spoken of, since it is also referred to in this way.[43] I cannot see how this omission can be explained in any way which would help to throw more light on the method of composition of the saga; it is surely a blemish of workmanship which attracts our attention merely because of the close-knit composition of the story. By examining the saga closely along these lines we are more likely to be able to decide whether it resembles in form and content those sagas which we have best reason to believe are based on raw material drawn from oral tradition.

IV

COMPOSITION AND METHOD OF NARRATION

INDISPUTABLY *Hrafnkatla* is the most coherent and neatly constructed of all the Icelandic sagas. From the early moment when it begins to describe the power and pride of Hrafnkell the events follow each other like links in a delicately constructed chain: Hrafnkell's solemn vow, Einarr's blunder and his slaying, the offer of atonement to Thorbjǫrn and his refusal of it, Sámr's acceptance of the lawsuit (after the slaying) which appears to be hopeless, the unexpected assistance of the sons of Thjóstarr which because of Hrafnkell's carelessness leads to his downfall at the Althing and at home, his humiliation and second rise to power, the slaying of Eyvindr, Hrafnkell's resumption of his rightful position and his complete discomfiture of Sámr. Then Sámr's forlorn attempt to get assistance, its rejection, Hrafnkell's death, and the end of the saga. The thread is held firmly and without digression, so that the saga closely resembles those *Þættir* [short tales] which have been constructed with the greatest care (*Auðunar þáttr vestfirzka*, for example), and no other saga equals it in this respect. The two sagas which are most nearly comparable to it, *Hænsa-Þóris saga* and *Bandamanna saga*, are both short and clearly presented. If we set ourselves the task of retelling these three sagas after one reading in order to include everything that is essential to the story, it would become obvious that it is easiest to give the outline of *Hrafnkatla*. *Hænsa-Þóris saga* would still retain its unity if we omitted the unsuccessful attempt of Thorbjǫrn stígandi to seek the support of Oddr of Tongue after the burning, or the dealings between Oddr and Gunnarr Hlífarson after the conclusion of the lawsuit at the Althing. Despite its skilful construction *Bandamanna saga* shows signs of having been strung together from smaller tales which originally were composed independ-

Composition and Method of Narration

ently, though the joining is cleverly done. The link between the quarrels of Oddr Ófeigsson and the legal proceedings of the confederates against Oddr is far less strongly made than the connexion between Sámr's difficulties at the Althing and the support of the sons of Thjóstarr, which is so skilfully woven into the action of *Hrafnkatla*. Hermundr Illugason's death was unnecessary for the story; there is no similar superfluity in our saga. It would be even easier to demonstrate the superior unity and finish of construction in *Hrafnkatla* if we were to select for comparison any sagas other than these two—a gratuitous exercise for those who know the Family Sagas. In this respect two other sagas from the Austfirðir, *Vápnfirðinga saga* and *Droplaugarsona saga*, would repay further study: they are older than *Hrafnkatla*, and are thought to be based on ancient oral tradition.

At this point it would be well to mention one excellent trait in the construction of the saga: the method of dealing with a single or double-stranded narrative when two stories are being unfolded simultaneously but neither can be carried through immediately to its proper conclusion. After Einarr releases Freyfaxi and sees him rush off down the dale, he tries unsuccessfully to catch him. At that moment Einarr must have known that his own death was near. But we are not told his fears or whether he thinks of escape. The saga follows the horse. Einarr is not mentioned again until Hrafnkell meets him as he lies idly on the wall of the sheepfold counting his sheep. He has not attempted to flee from danger any more than he thinks to avoid telling the truth. This is very effective and makes his slaying appear all the more deplorable.

A similar method is used in the account of Hrafnkell's ride to the General Assembly. We follow him south to Síða. He arrives at the Assembly after Sámr, is informed of Sámr's arrival and thinks it amusing. After this we learn nothing of his behaviour until Sámr brings the case against him before the court. 'Men rushed to Hrafnkell's booth and told him what was about to happen.' This silence shows best what Hrafnkell thinks of

Sámr's antics, and how he discounts them; at the same time it explains how his careless contempt allowed his own affairs to drift beyond any apparent point of recovery.

One curious use of the two-strand method must surely be considered a defect of craftsmanship. After Hrafnkell's humiliation at Aðalból the Saga describes his purchase of land and his rise to power in the first *years* at Hrafnkelsstaðir. After returning to describe events at Aðalból in the first *days* after Hrafnkell's departure, it *then* describes Hrafnkell's reception of the reports about the destruction of Freyfaxi and the temple-burning—events which, of course, took place a few days after his departure. It would have been more natural if the saga had told first of Hrafnkell's departure, then of the activities of Sámr and the sons of Thjóstarr, followed by Hrafnkell's reception of the news, and in this way had avoided splitting in two the section describing his second rise to power. Such an arrangement would have had the additional merit of resembling more closely the method of narration employed in popular oral recitation. We are left with the feeling that the author could not part from Hrafnkell until the reader had been assured of what his ultimate fate would be, and also that he wanted to make his comment on the gods directly after the destruction of Freyfaxi and the temple without any intervening account of Hrafnkell's new establishment.

Hrafnkatla conceals much of its art on a first reading, and closer scrutiny can give rise to many surprises: for instance, the number of different subjects brought before the reader in such a short reading time. Not only does the saga give Hrafnkell's biography from youth to death and trace his life with its violent vicissitudes in external fortune and great changes of temperament, it also gives a clear account of the fates and foibles of various other men. Even so, the saga is never a mere dry survey: there always appears to be room for detailed accounts of major or minor occurrences. At the end of the saga the reader feels that he has lived through it all; on occasions he has even been astonished at the thoroughness with which the material has been

Composition and Method of Narration

sifted and expounded, so that when he reaches the last paragraph and reads 'Finis' he can scarcely believe that all this could have been conveyed to him in so few pages.

We must now try to discover how this effect has been achieved. One element in the choice of material is always vastly important in our ancient sagas: how many men are dealt with and how they are described. As we all know, the biographical complexities in most sagas are a serious stumbling-block to modern readers, confusing them and dissipating their attention, so that it is not easy for them to hold the thread of the narrative or get to the heart of the story.

Twenty-five characters are named in *Hrafnkatla*. Seven of these appear in the first chapter alone—the ancestors of Haraldr hárfagri and the female slave Arnthrúðr, all of whom have nothing to do with the main story. Similarly, Thormóðr Thjóstarsson and Thórdís Thórólfsdóttir are merely named in passing, and it was necessary to name Hrafnkell's father, his wife, and his sons (four names). Then we have the sons of Hallsteinn and Hrólfr who are mentioned among Hrafnkell's men at the pursuit of Eyvindr (four names). In all, this gives seventeen characters who are mere names. There remain eight persons (plus two unnamed subsidiary characters, the serving-woman and the *skósveinn*) who really contribute to the story's development: Hrafnkell, Bjarni, Sámr, Eyvindr, Thorbjǫrn, Einarr, Thorkell, Thorgeirr. With these eight pieces the game is played and each of them is clearly described. Such economy in the number of characters is unique in the Icelandic sagas, even though we compare *Hrafnkatla* with *Víglundar saga* or *Króka-Refs saga*, where there was no oral tradition to lead the authors into this particular temptation.

The saga is much more lavish with place-names. There are seventy in all. As a rule the proportion is reversed: there are more names of people than of places. But *Hrafnkatla* displays a considerable conscientiousness in recording and explaining place-names; and, as was shown above, scholars who otherwise believe this saga to be derived from oral tradition see in this trait the hand of an author. Some of the points referred to earlier (see Chapter II) suggest that not only was the author fond of old place-names but that he liked to use them for his particular artistic purpose: in them he finds material for his story, from them he invents characters and fabricates incidents; further, he is able to point to them in confirmation of his story. For, of course, like all the authors of the old sagas and even of the sagas of the earliest days (*Fornaldarsǫgur*),[44] he wanted as much trust as possible placed in his saga. And this object he has achieved with astonishing success down to the present day.

The derivations of place-names given in the saga show that, although the author always kept the main theme of the saga clearly before him and knew how to control and limit his material, he does not maintain this economy pedantically (see, for instance, the introduction into Chapter I of men who are quite unnecessary to the main action). Let me further demonstrate how he indulged personal interests beyond the strict demands of his story. The explanation of legal terms is a particular feature of the saga. 'No man is outlawed until the court of execution has been held and that must take place at his own domicile fourteen nights after the taking up of weapons when everyone rides away from the Thing.' 'Will you go away with Sámr outside the home-meadow within an arrow-shot from the house, and hold the court of execution on some rocky mound where there is neither ploughed land nor level pasture. This must be done when the sun is due south.' Clearly, these are passages taken from the law-books.[45]

Occasionally quite superfluous explanations of men's actions and innermost thoughts are recorded, a practice which as a rule is used sparingly in the ancient sagas: '[Einarr] seemed to think that he would be carried along the faster if he rode instead of walking'; 'but in the firm belief that the future was dark for the man who brings down on himself the curse for a broken vow, he leapt at him from horseback and gave him his death-blow'; 'now he had gone to sleep afterwards and had stretched out his foot over the footboard because of the excessive heat which he had had in the foot'; 'because of this old Hallfreðr took the lower paths although they were the longer'. Many other instances could be found, especially in the conversations with which we shall deal later.

The saga's descriptions of incidents are not lengthy but they are very precise and sometimes unnecessarily detailed: for example, the account of old Thorbjǫrn's visit to Sámr. 'He now rides away (from Laugarhús). . . . He does not stop before he comes down to Leikskálar, knocks there on the door. The door is answered. Thorbjǫrn asks Sámr to come outside. Sámr greets his kinsman heartily', &c. For an example of exceptionally clear description we may refer to the story of Freyfaxi and Einarr. The weather is described on this fateful morning; 'Einarr went out early and then all the mist from the south and the drizzle had lifted'—the pursuit of the horses—Einarr's journey—Freyfaxi's appearance after the ride—'the horse was dripping with sweat so that it ran from every hair; he was badly mud-splashed and exceedingly tired'. Later this is repeated— 'very dirty . . . very filthy'. Often trifling details are given without any cogent reason for dotting the 'i's and crossing the 't's: Sámr and Thorbjǫrn go outside and down *below the bridge*; Thorkell had a light lock of hair *on the left side*. Numerals are given without hesitation: Hrafnkell rides to the General Assembly with 70 men; Thorgeirr has 70 men there; Hrafnkell attacks Sámr with 70 men; Sámr has 40 men at the Assembly, and Thorgeirr selects 40 from his force of Westfirthers. When they arrive at Aðalból 20 men guard the horses and 60 rush the house. Eyvindr rides with 5 men who drive 16 pack-horses; Hrafnkell pursues Eyvindr with 17 men and Sámr rides to his brother's aid with 19 others. We are even told how many times Freyfaxi rolled over, 'some dozen times'. Thorkell has been abroad for 7 years, Eyvindr for 7, and Sámr remains at Aðalból for 6 years.

All this description, explanation, and close attention to trifles —and many more examples of the same kind could be produced —gives a reader the comfortable feeling that there has been no irresponsible handling of the subject-matter, nor has the evidence for the saga's incidents been ignored. But above everything else, the conversations recorded in the saga are so presented that we seem to be living the story and gain the impression that the narration is thorough, although such a vast amount of material is covered in so short a space.

For its size *Hrafnkatla* has relatively more conversation than most of the sagas about Icelanders, and at times its characters are so long-winded that they seem to be discoursing rather than conversing.[46] Hrafnkell's offer of terms of reconciliation to Thorbjǫrn is made in twenty-two continuous lines; the talk between Sámr and Thorkell at the Assembly and the subsequent conversation with Thorgeirr in the booth is nearly 130 lines; the serving-woman's outburst against Hrafnkell is twelve lines, and Hrafnkell's arbitration award with Sámr twenty lines. If we remember that in Cawley's edition (which is the basis for these calculations) the saga is 950 lines long we can see how much is told through the conversations. They are used to give us the impression that we are listening to the main events of the saga even while these are being enacted, and that we know the characters so intimately that their very silences are eloquent—like Einarr saying nothing when Freyfaxi escapes from his control, or Hrafnkell remaining silent while he is being outlawed at the General Assembly. The reader becomes so engrossed in the story that involuntarily he fills in gaps where the story gathers most speed. In fact, the effect is that of drama, and *Hrafnkatla* exhibits this characteristic of the best plays, that portrayal of character takes precedence over everything else. This theme must be considered further in a separate chapter.

Before doing so we must comment a little on the author's style. On the whole it is pithy, as one can expect when so large a subject is compressed into such a small compass. Numerous phrases conjure up vivid pictures: 'who carried more bone in their fists', 'who might row faster across the bay than Hrafnkell', 'I fancy his "helmet of terror" will overshadow most people once more', 'I cannot remain friendly with you right to the tip of the blade', 'for then the prey will not be in the snare' [*en þá er eigi dýr í festi*],⁴⁷ 'under the guidance of our oars'. Proverbs are rather numerous and we are sometimes told that they are taken from the people: 'this is an old proverb'; 'now many will recall the old saying'; 'that is mostly true which was said of old'. Many examples could be given which show how skilfully proverbs are used to give insight into character: as in the case of Bjarni of Laugarhús and of Thorkell lepp.

This author, who knows so well how to achieve contrast in characterization, shows a corresponding use of balance in his style: '*Eigi veldr* ástleysi *þessarri brottkvaðning — meira veldr því* efnaleysi *mitt ok fátœkt*'; '*þú ert* gjarn á smásakar, *en villt eigi taka við* þessu *máli, er svá er brynt*'; '*muntu þess mest* á þér *kenna, — mun hann þess gørst kenna* á sér'; '*Er honum þetta* nauðsyn, *en eigi* seiling'. Again, Eyvindr rides with so bright a shield that the sun's rays gleam from it, but Hrafnkell and his men (the pursuers) arm themselves grimly in battle-fashion. The issue of the fight is adumbrated in this choice of epithets.

We are constantly made aware that the author had a sharp eye for the *mot juste*, although he does not make the mistake of using it to excess. One example will serve for many. Hrafnkell is rarely called 'godi' in the saga; the first occasion (except when his surname is given in Chapter II) is during Sámr's search for help from the principal men at the General Assembly: 'but no one declared that he had so much to repay Sámr that he wanted to become involved in a lawsuit against Hrafnkell godi'. The use of Hrafnkell's full title at this point emphasizes Sámr's plight: how could he, a man without power, expect other chieftains to support *him* against one of their number? The word is next used by Sámr himself in conversation with Thorkell: 'we have a dispute to settle with Hrafnkell godi'. This is no purely formal introduction of Hrafnkell—his father's name and his place of residence would have been sufficient for that; at one and the same time it echoes the answers which Sámr had previously received from the other chieftains, and shows too that

Sámr likes the sound of it in his own mouth—Behold, I am waging a struggle against one of the mighty men in the land!

A similar effect is gained by Thorkell when he persuades his brother to change his mind about supporting Sámr: 'It may be that Thorkell lepp will come to that place where his word carries more weight.' This reference to himself in the third person and with his own nickname (used only this once in the saga) conveys the effect of Thorkell regarding himself from a distance and feeling all the more annoyed at his present lack of power. It is obvious how much flatter would be the sentence, 'if *I* should come there', &c.

At times, one cannot deny it, the style is a little long-winded, and Finnur Jónsson noted that it fell short of the saga's skilful composition.[48] Many of the longer speeches would have been equally effective if they had been shorter and less prone to explain a speaker's intentions: for example, the outburst of the serving-woman and Hrafnkell's offer to Thorbjǫrn when he says 'but we must often repent this that we are too talkative, and seldom would we have to repent if we spoke less than more . . . I feel that this slaying is among the worst that I have done . . . this slaying seems to me the worst of those I have done.' Such repetitions are common: 'I have sworn a compelling oath about this. . . . Do now as I say. . . . Now that you know what I have sworn.' 'You will then have something or other for your suffering, some comfort or humiliation more than before, and either disgrace or sorrow.' '(Hrafnkell) was gentle and good-natured with his own men but harsh and stubborn with the men of Jǫkulsdalr.'

In this regard one suspects that the saga occasionally reveals a trace of the learned, ecclesiastical style, though this rarely appears in the choice of vocabulary. Perhaps we could indicate the use of *linr* instead of *mildur* and of *náungi* for *frændi*, but these are not enough to suggest a clerical status for the author. My opinion is that the style indicates a gifted author who had steeped himself in the native Icelandic historical writers but did not command the ease of style of the great masters. The

Composition and Method of Narration

style of saga writing developed gradually from two kinds of narration. The one was the primitive narrative style of oral tradition of which we get a fair idea from the so-called *Ættasǫgur* of the Norwegians and from some folk tales of later times written down by Icelandic commoners who had been uninfluenced by any literary education. Their treatment of the subject-matter is abrupt, often inept, with wooden conversations; those readers who are conversant with a more polished and detailed narrative style seem to feel that the story is merely like a précis—though really it never had any other form. The second influence was the foreign clerical style, broad, complicated, and sweeping. Both from their knowledge of literary Latin style and through translations from it into Icelandic after c. 1100, the Icelanders succeeded in creating their own narrative style from these two opposites and in uniting much of the simplicity of everyday speech with the copiousness of the literary language. In some of the earliest sagas it is apparent that the authors have not fused these components successfully together. In *Heiðarvíga saga*, for example, there are striking differences in the style adopted for various chapters. The plans of Thórarinn spaki and the southern journeys, described in laborious detail, are followed by the bald account of Barði's journey north after the slaying. It is as if a bare rock stands out on a fertile plain. The bareness is not due to erosion: it has never been covered. It reads as though the author had become exhausted by his great effort in the preceding exposition and was now glad for a time to allow material from oral tradition to stand forth in all its crudity. During the course of the thirteenth century a nicer balance was achieved. Snorri, who based his Kings' Sagas on many older sources with heterogeneous styles, left behind him a powerful example. He had shortened and expanded at will, and had stripped from the Lives of the Saints their vestments of learned style and clothed them in a simpler yet more becoming dress, while at the same time he smartened up the fustian of poorer, less elegantly expressed sources to make them match with the literary style of the rest. It is more or less clear to us—and would be still more apparent had we some of the older sagas in their original forms, not shortened and mutilated by later writers (cf. the texts of *Egils saga* and *Glúms saga* in *Möðruvallabók* and *Fóstbrœðra saga* in *Hauksbók*)—that the development of the saga style in the thirteenth and fourteenth centuries was in the direction of giving the sagas an 'oral' quality. This has led scholars astray in more recent times. Obviously such a style would in practice produce stories which were most suited for recitation. Possibly, too, the best educated writers may well have trained themselves to tell stories in this way (as, for example, Sturla Thórðarson had learned to tell the Saga of Huld), and many other authors may have practised reciting whole sagas or chapters of sagas which they were engaged in composing. But the saga style is still as far from what the primitive oral style can have been before the Age of Writing as it was from the daily speech of the thirteenth century which occasionally peeps through the narrative in *Sturlunga*. The supreme achievement of literary art is to make books 'talk' and few succeed in reaching it. Incredible though it may seem, it is nevertheless true that in the full flowering of saga-writing the nearer the Sagas approximated to the modern ideal of spoken narrative, the closer they came to being the work of an author, that is, at once more independent of the oral tradition and of the crutches of foreign stylistic models.

This kind of stylistic evolution, like any other literary and cultural manifestation, is never as constant in its progress as is the process of growth and decay among species governed by natural laws. A pattern does emerge clearly from a survey over a long period, but when individual ability and local conditions are also considered, it becomes difficult to assign any particular work to its precise point in the development. Men appear who are before or after their day: pioneers, geniuses, men of refined taste who struggle against a lowering standard, and backward writers who, at any given moment, do not know how to avail themselves of the new symbols of their art.[49]

Even when the speed of narration is greatest, the style of

Composition and Method of Narration

Hrafnkatla never seems to me to use the primitive oral narrative methods of popular tradition which in places are so clearly adopted in the older sagas from the Austfirðir, *Droplaugarsona saga* and *Vápnfirðinga saga*. But there are traces of influence from the learned style although only a few marks of its restricting bonds remain. The fully developed Icelandic saga style is used generally in this saga, and yet it is being composed in a district which was remote from the main centres of saga composition by a man who has perhaps written nothing else—at least, nothing that has come down to us. A case could be made out for saying that this saga was written in a style which was a little behind and not ahead of its time, and that it was written late in the century; a conclusion which agrees with other indications of its date of composition.

V

CHARACTERIZATION

WE have already said that there are only eight effective characters in the saga. Each possesses his idiosyncracies, but the detail with which each is portrayed varies directly with his part in the story.

In the main Einarr Thorbjarnarson is presented to us as a pawn of fate. His father does not inform him that he must find a job until well into the Spring. Because of this he has no choice but to tend sheep although he is an accomplished young man. He now has the favourite Freyfaxi (the horse he has been forbidden to ride) before his eyes throughout the summer. Anyone who has experienced the joy of riding a good horse knows what a temptation this must be to an Icelandic country lad. For a long time he stands up to the test. Then, finally, when he desperately needs a horse, and as if by magic all the others have become wild, Freyfaxi almost begs to be ridden. He can contain himself no longer. He rides the horse a very long way—to look for ewes which all the time were grazing quite near to the shieling. Once Freyfaxi has escaped to Aðalból Einarr knows that he is doomed. But he makes no attempt to escape and only tries to postpone the inevitable by first telling Hrafnkell of his bad luck with the missing ewes. Hrafnkell kills him at once and with this Einarr's part in the saga is over. It was unnecessary to make more of his character. The despotism of the Fates has been revealed. His misdeed is so trivial that the arrogant Hrafnkell feels that slaying him is one of his worst acts. Yet we know enough about Einarr to sympathize the more readily with Thorbjǫrn's feelings; not only had he to seek legal redress for a son's death: that son was a brave and promising young man.

There is a striking similarity between Einarr and his first cousin, Eyvindr Bjarnason, who also falls at Hrafnkell's hands. Eyvindr, though, has a wealthy father and does not have to look for a job; he makes journeys to foreign parts and becomes a man of some substance. His fate is due to the quarrel between his brother Sámr and Hrafnkell. Eyvindr is no fool. When he learns of Sámr's new prosperity he says little about it, as though he feels that this season of ease and plenty must be short-lived. But he will not flee before Hrafnkell because he knows that he has done him no harm; it is not his nature to think ill of men until he has tested their intentions, nor will he allow his own reputation for courage to be stained. He defends himself courageously against odds and is killed. This is the difference between his death and that of his cousin: Einarr is slain defenceless by his employer just like a beast, while Eyvindr defends himself, killing some of Hrafnkell's men though he cannot overcome Hrafnkell himself.

The portrayal of the two brothers Bjarni of Laugarhús and Thorbjǫrn of Hóll is a study in strong contrasts. Bjarni controls a great deal of money but lives a moderate life. Having no fond conceits about playing the champion against powerful chieftains, he denies support to his brother and in no way interferes in the lawsuit although his son Sámr is engaged in it up to the hilt. His motto is, 'He is a wise man who knows his own limitations'. Thorbjǫrn has little wealth but many dependants; yet there is an element of pride in him. He refuses the excellent offer which Hrafnkell makes to him for the slaying of his son Einarr because he cannot stomach the idea of Hrafnkell's making the award. He wishes other men to act as arbitrators between them. When Hrafnkell will not accede to this, Thorbjǫrn urges first Bjarni and then Sámr to take up the case against him. It is only at the Althing that his spirit deserts him and he realizes that the task is too much for him. Then he breaks down and weeps. Undoubtedly the author portrays him sympathetically, for he never becomes a figure of fun. There is a complete understanding of his sorrow and pride, though his poverty restrains him from the full exercise of that quickness of passion which is, in fact, part of his true nature.

The principal character in the saga is without question that of

Hrafnkell goði. A despotic man accustomed from early childhood to having his own way, he has succeeded in everything he has attempted and has always been blest with good luck. To him it is a source of mirth that Sámr should have taken over the lawsuit against him and that he should ride to the Althing to carry on with its prosecution. He ignores the proceedings at the Althing until it is too late. After the verdict he rides home, an outlaw in name, as though nothing has happened. Not for one moment does it enter his head that any attempt will be made to carry out the sentence; he neglects to place a guard around the farm and sleeps late on the very morning that his enemies arrive at Aðalból. He is unpopular, and most men are pleased that at last he has received a fitting punishment for his many injustices.

Arrogance is not, however, the only element in his character. It is recorded that he was gentle and good-natured with his own men (that is, those of his own dependants to whom he had given land in Hrafnkelsdalr itself). He intensely dislikes having to kill Einarr and offers Thorbjǫrn a princely settlement for him; the terms of the offer are given in detail and show both his compassion and thoughtfulness. It is necessary that these good qualities should be displayed early in the saga if the reader is to become reconciled to his ultimate prosperity. One trait, however, must be clearly understood not only in the temperament of Hrafnkell but also in the pride of every chieftain of the Old Republic: he cannot tolerate the idea of allowing one of his common thingmen to submit a dispute between them to outside arbitration.

Before Hrafnkell slays Einarr there are two courses open to him, both distasteful: either he must break the powerful oath he has sworn, or he must kill a servant he likes for a mere trifle. This dramatic situation is not uncommon in our ancient literature, both in the Eddic poetry and in the sagas; fate can drive men into such desperate corners that a foul deed can appear the better of two evils. Bolli must slay Kjartan his sworn foster-brother, Gísli Súrsson his brother-in-law Thorgrímr; Flosi must burn Njáll and Bergthóra in their home. Yet, knowing that their actions are evil, men who are truly great choose and act without hesitation.

The choice which Sámr offers Hrafnkell is even more difficult: to accept death or a life of disgrace, dishonour, and defeat. According to the creed of the Heroic Age honour was the test of a man's worth. The sense of honour, the refusal to accept insult, these were the very stuff of the events with which the sagas deal and which elevated the petty quarrels into momentous conflicts Yet, chiefly because of his sons, Hrafnkell chose life that he might bring them to man's estate. This also suggests that he has absolute trust in his own ability to redress the balance later and thus rid himself of any stigma of shame. He chose the more difficult course in complete defiance of the heroic code of his age.

Under this new kind of ordeal his character develops and his nature takes on new qualities: 'He had now gained more control over his temper. The man was more popular than before; he had the same readiness to help and showed the same hospitality, but he was much more friendly now and quieter and gentler in every way than before.' He has tamed his violence of temper and behaves with moderation. This is shown unmistakably when he has to settle with Sámr. He makes a judgement which, according to the circumstances of the case, is both fair and proper. But his chastening acquaintance with overwhelming opposition has made him cautious and cruel at the same time. Accepting the saga's account of his second rise to power and prosperity at Hrafnkelsstaðir, he could not have had long to wait before he was ready and able to create some opportunity for getting even with Sámr. Instead he continued to wait. He knew that Sámr's brother, Eyvindr, was abroad and was likely to become a man of power and distinction when he returned to Iceland; Hrafnkell could not risk his returning and (by a flank attack) avenging his brother, Sámr. This interpretation of Hrafnkell's delay is presented quite clearly in the words of Thorgeirr Thjóstarsson to Sámr: 'It is now clear what a difference of judgement distinguishes you from Hrafnkell, since he allowed you to remain in peace and attacked when, in his view, the more dangerous brother appeared on the scene.' Above everything else the slaying of Eyvindr is a safety measure. Hrafnkell removes the only man from whom effective revenge can be expected, before he commits the one deed which can lay him open to the possibility of revenge, i.e. the resumption of his old power at Sámr's expense. When Eyvindr is dead he feels so safe that he can afford to be merciful. He shows moderation, too, by not seeking vengeance against the sons of Thjóstarr although they had done him great wrong. In this there is a tacit recognition that his earlier conduct had not been blameless and that they had punished him for his pride and cruelty. Besides, the brothers lived so far away that revenge would be difficult and hazardous. After the slaying of Eyvindr he flees before Sámr without feeling any shame. He does not wish to place himself in further jeopardy. Eyvindr could not permit himself to flee from Hrafnkell. He has not dignity enough to do 'what most men would consider contemptible'. Hrafnkell, however, is prepared to run away because, at last, complete rehabilitation is within his reach. This time he does not sleep late. Sámr summons his men for the next morning; Hrafnkell gathers his men that evening, marches west across the heath during the night, and seizes Sámr in his bed.

Hrafnkell's ferocity is shown in the slaying of Eyvindr against whom he had no direct quarrel. 'He had no word to say to Eyvindr but went straight into the attack.' He does not stop until Eyvindr and all his fellows are dead. 'That was well and truly done.' This time he shows no remorse, as he did after Einarr's death. As he tells Sámr: 'For Eyvindr your brother there shall be no award because you prosecuted the case so ruthlessly for your former kinsman.'

Rarely indeed in the Family Sagas is the development of a man's character portrayed as thoroughly as it is here; rarely does an author show so unmistakably that he knows what he is about. Snorri Sturluson attains this ideal in *Ólafs saga helga* where from two distinct descriptions of a man he shapes anew the whole character in order to demonstrate how experience and adversity can make a saint out of a turbulent viking.[50] To discover whether the author of *Hrafnkatla* had known Snorri's work would be a difficult task, but there is a most striking similarity to Snorri's method of character portrayal in the way he employs contrasting types: Bjarni and Thorbjǫrn, Hrafnkell and Sámr, and, above all, Thorgeirr and Thorkell. Neither would I care to state dogmatically that he knew *Heiðarvíga saga* and *Eyrbyggja*, and yet, significantly, Víga-Styrr and Snorri godi spring to mind in comparison with Hrafnkell. At the beginning of the saga we hear of Hrafnkell that 'he entered a great deal into single conflicts and would pay no man compensation'. *Eyrbyggja* says of Styrr: 'He slew many men in duels and paid compensation for none'. This is a kind of reference to *Heiðarvíga saga* which relates in much detail the particular slayings of Styrr. It seems obvious that the author of *Hrafnkatla* had no information about the earlier slayings by Hrafnkell, and it is very unlikely that such a chieftain would have fought duels instead of using the power of his men. In his high temper and injustice Styrr is not so complex a character as Hrafnkell; we need only compare his sneering words about the grey lamb to the hapless Gestr Thórhallsson with Hrafnkell's proffered settlement after Einarr's slaying to see the difference between them. Even so, Styrr may have been a prototype for this aspect of Hrafnkell's character, though the description has been modified because the author wished to show a maturer development. In his old age Hrafnkell is remarkably like Snorri godi: he displays the same caution, moderation, and cruelty. Neither is shown in any heroic light. Thus Hrafnkell pursues Eyvindr's five men with eighteen and after losing twelve of them he flees before Sámr. But in the description of each of them there is a feeling of coldness tinged with a certain amount of admiration. Such similarities may be mere chance, but it is natural enough that a saga which is a complete work of fiction, as *Hrafnkatla* is, should reveal directly or indirectly some things which it owes to older sagas based on historical events.

Sámr is portrayed with a slightly humorous touch, although the author also feels kindly disposed towards him. He is not insignificant; he has courage and daring, he thinks a great deal of his honour and has sufficient pride to refuse the gifts of the sons of Thjóstarr when they deny him support at the end of the saga. Unfortunately he is not born to be a chieftain. His elevation to that rank is a trick of fortune which he cannot adapt to his own needs. For this task he lacks intelligence, practical common sense, and consistency of purpose. When he has won his case at the Althing he is perfectly happy, though his victory is only nominal. 'Since I am asked, it seems to me that Hrafnkell has received a snub which will be long remembered ... and that is worth more than money.' He lacks the ruthlessness necessary to take Hrafnkell's life when he has him in his power, not realizing that he will never be secure against Hrafnkell after their clash together. He treats Hrafnkell exactly as Sturla Sighvatsson deals with Gizurr at Álptavatn. At one and the same time he goes too far and yet not far enough. He is warned: 'You will repent this the most that you have given him his life'. Sámr says that he could not help it. This is instinctive behaviour on his part. Later Thorgeirr reminds him of both his folly and his lucklessness. Thorgeirr had warned him to be on his guard 'because it is not easy to deal with an evil man'. Even after this warning Sámr has not sense enough to fear for himself. He behaves handsomely in his new position of authority, but his character does not mature in prosperity as Hrafnkell's does in adversity.

Like many a man whose ambition exceeds his ability, Sámr bridges the gap between his dreams and reality by a show of considerable self-importance. The author frequently pokes fun at this. Old Thorbjǫrn says to Sámr: 'You are the most boisterous man in our family'. Sámr is very proud of his legal knowledge: 'We need the backing of chieftains, but as for the pleading of the case, that will be safe in my hands.' Although prudence counselled concealment once he had been promised assistance, he does not know how to hide his delight. After his victorious lawsuit he walks about the Althing 'strutting like a peacock'. Thorgeirr points out to him how difficult his relationship with

Characterization

Hrafnkell will be back in their own district. 'I do not care for that', says Sámr. 'You are a bold fellow', is Thorgeirr's reply, but the implication is that Sámr is a fool.

The sons of Thjóstarr are sketched with a few bold strokes. Thorkell is brisk, goodhearted, inexperienced, eager for risky enterprises, and anxious to court danger. ('Nothing ventured, nothing gained' is his motto.) Thorgeirr is circumspect, staid, slow to undertake anything, but fearless once he lets himself go, realistic and merciless. Their portrayal is so clear-cut that in one place it is possible to emend the text of the manuscripts on this evidence alone. In view of their natures it must be Thorgeirr and not Thorkell who warns Sámr against giving Hrafnkell his life. This is confirmed later in the saga when Thorgeirr says to Sámr: 'It has gone exactly as I thought . . . that you would repent this the most'.

The strangest incident in the saga is Thorkell's plan for ensuring the success of Thorbjǫrn's request for help—that he should get in touch with Thorgeirr by roughly seizing his damaged foot while he is asleep, and then awaiting the consequences. Thorbjǫrn thinks this is foolish counsel, and many readers too have found neither rhyme nor reason in it. But the author of *Hrafnkatla* knows what he is about at all times, and never more so than here.

Reflect for a moment on the relationship between the two brothers and their contrasting natures as these have been shown to us at this stage in the story. Ever since they were lads the younger, Thorkell, has brought forward proposals for great and small projects which they should undertake, but the elder, Thorgeirr, has persistently poured cold water on these schemes. The difference of character has been heightened since Thorkell's foreign travel, single, ever impressionable and eager for adventure as he is, while Thorgeirr stays at home maintaining the farm and their joint authority, becoming daily more cautious and conservative in the light of everyday experience. Thorkell has been itching to upset the balanced composure of this worldly-wise man. Words would be insufficient to effect it; they would be as waves which lash themselves into foam against this rock of reason and taciturnity. But now there is one weak chink in Thorgeirr's armour; his toe is excruciatingly painful. If, at this moment, someone were to give it a fierce tug, increasing the agony, and if, at the same time, Thorgeirr could be roused into a towering passion, then it might be possible to play on his natural feelings and make him for a while abandon his insufferable circumspection. It is easier to sway a man from one emotion to another than it is to kindle enthusiasm out of Laodicean indifference. There was no hope of getting Thorgeirr to do anything so absurd as helping a mere rustic Eastfirther against his godi (a dangerous opponent) by mere sensible arguments; the better way was to let him first blaze up in real anger and then wait for the inevitable reaction. There was a risk, of course, but Thorkell was eager to take it. He sweeps into the booth as Thorgeirr is waking from his bad dream and begins talking. At first Thorgeirr makes the obvious retort that he has not killed the old man's son and does not deserve to have it revenged on his toe. Thorkell keeps rattling on, playing all his cards against his brother until he has gained his point.

The situation is very different in the account of Sámr's visit to their home at the end of the saga. Thorkell is present, but 'this time Thorgeirr did all the answering for the brothers'. Thorkell says nothing, whatever he may be thinking. This time Thorgeirr is completely himself and listens to Sámr with polite yet ice-cold detachment.

A lengthy discussion as to whether such characters belong to fiction or to orally preserved tradition should be unnecessary. Sir Walter Scott has finely drawn the distinction which he observed between true oral narrative and fictitious works of art:

> In actual life we come across many things which we cannot attribute to any everyday causes and origins, and if we had to draw the clearest distinction between true tales and fiction, we should say that a true story would be obscure, capable of many explanations, and mysterious when the most fundamental causes of it are sought, while in a work of fiction the author has to give a clear explanation

for the cause of all the incidents which he describes; in short, he has to explain everything.[51]

The characters in *Hrafnkatla* are presented with exceptional clarity. Although the author believes in fate there is always a perfect explanation for the actions of his characters in their actual natures and temperaments. Incidents develop from human failings so that often we cannot say what is due to fate and what is self-caused. The characters live out their own lives; they are not puppets in the author's hands as they are in schoolboy fiction. Yet they never get out of control, with the result that there is nothing about them obscure, incredible, or incongruous. It is as though every deed and word had been carefully weighed and precisely assigned by the economy of art. The insight into the characters' development, acutely revealing their hidden depths, is far in advance of the disjointed and simple portrayals of character in the folk sagas and oral tales. The subject-matter which has been selected for the story has been so artistically disposed and is employed so economically that the reader feels that he has been allowed to read a full biography, though, actually, he has been offered a single chapter in a life. So much is poured into that one chapter that all the principal qualities and fortunes of the major and minor characters are clearly presented. This is the technique of a branch of fiction which is rarer than either the novel or the short story. What an interesting separate study it would be to compare the excellences of this saga with the technique of some of the most famous works in this *genre*, for example, Kleist's *Michael Kohlhaus*. I believe it would then become clearer, when the arguments for and against each work had been thoroughly sifted, that *Hrafnkatla* is one of the most completely developed 'short novels' in world literature.

VI

FINDINGS AND CONCLUSIONS

THE findings which arise from the above observations may now be stated briefly.

Hrafnkell's expulsion from Aðalból, his second rise to power at Hrafnkelsstaðir, his subsequent resumption of his previous authority, in fact all the principal events in the saga, never took place. Two of the chief actors, the sons of Thjóstarr, never existed. Many other details of some importance, Hrafnkell's descent, his rise to authority and the name of his farm, the lawsuit against Einarr being taken direct to the Althing *et al.*, are shown (after comparison with more trustworthy sources) to be inaccurate as they are presented in the saga. Other things which cannot be tested against existing sources—the slaying of Einarr and Eyvindr, and what is said in general about these two cousins—are so closely linked with the fictitious subject-matter that they cannot command belief as they stand without further evidence. In fact it would be contrary to common sense and experience to maintain a belief in the minor events after the major ones had been disproved. For example, if we should cease to believe that the Burning of Njáll ever took place, would it not be foolish to assert that many of the statements made about the causes and the effects of the burning were based on historically true events, but in connexion with an entirely different burning? On the contrary, most people nowadays would agree that though the burning indisputably took place much of what the saga says about its details is unreliable. Once we have admitted that a Hrafnkell and his sons existed but that Króka-Refr did not, there is little difference between *Hrafnkatla* and *Króka-Refs saga* as *historical* sources, though the former is a better and more realistic work of *fiction*.

The saga nowhere refers to oral tradition, never shows the slightest trace of having been derived from oral tales, and in

Findings and Conclusions

composition and the treatment of sources is most unlike those sagas which are supposed to follow popular tradition. There is good reason to assume that the author deliberately turned away from some sources which he knew and must have considered to be trustworthy—in other words, that the truth of his story was no concern of the author. In style, manner of narration, and portrayal of character, *Hrafnkatla* bears all the marks of a distinguished novel. Those who wish to maintain that it follows the pattern of oral tradition must choose between these alternatives: either to turn a blind eye to the art of this saga, its technical skill and profound understanding, or else to alter completely the current conceptions about folk-tales and their limitations, about the concerns and psychology of ordinary people. For a suitable comparison we need not turn aside to consider the *ættasǫgur* of the bookless Norse people; examples may be found among Icelandic tales of recent centuries, such as those which Gísli Konráðsson has committed to writing, whose tellers—and, even more, he himself—had, like their predecessors in this art, been familiar with the literature of seven uninterrupted centuries in addition to our ancient sagas, all of which should have assisted them in interpreting and shaping their material.

Thus it seems quite natural to believe, almost without any demonstration, that *Hrafnkatla* was the work of a single author whose purpose was not to narrate a true story but to compose a work of fiction; a man who, endowed with a powerful imagination, literary virtuosity, and a knowledge of men, was sustained by one of the most powerful literary movements in recorded history. He succeeded in creating a work which distils much of the quintessence of the Family Sagas at the height of their development, even though it is circumscribed by the limitations of this particular literary *genre*.

As to the author's personality, it is best not to go beyond those few clues to the nature of his ability and culture which can be deduced from the saga. Finnur Jónsson believed he was a cleric and seems to have based this opinion on the episode of the temple-burning and Hrafnkell's reception of the news. It is a doubtful assumption that in the latter half of the thirteenth century the Christian outlook which, except for this incident, is not prominent in the saga, should have been the special prerogative of the clergy, particularly since the rare examples of the learned style used in this saga give no indication of the author's status. More probably he was a man of substance, accustomed to legal disputes, observant and reflective, with an intimate knowledge (based on personal experience) of the necessary give and take, the pressure groups and lobbying inherent in the struggle for power. Almost certainly he knew Thingvellir, though he is not concerned to describe it, and I think it possible that he himself had taken the route to the Althing which in the saga Sámr is said to have taken. In all likelihood his home was in the district (probably in Fljótsdalr) in which the events of the saga took place, for when Hrafnkell goes to the Althing the time of the journey is recorded from Fljótsdalr to Thingvellir but not from Hrafnkelsdalr. He knew the southerly route from the Austfirðir to the Althing ('the usual route of thingmen from Síða') and the routes north across the country right up to Ljósavatnsskarð, and Sámr's route across the highlands. If he followed the route across 'the bridge', he would have seen (looking from Fljótsdalsheiðir to Aðalból) the site of the farm and the lanes but not the farm itself nor the lie of the ground beneath it down to the river. Apparently he never visited Hrafnkelsdalr itself, for everything that the saga says about its topography is either wrong or based on guesswork and the vague descriptions of other men's reports (e.g. what he says about Grjótteigssel and its surroundings).

The date of the saga can be determined by various probabilities. It must have been written after the end of the Republic [1262–4] and the introduction of the new law [1273]. The author carefully explains the old laws and judicial procedure to his readers, but he does this carelessly when he is not following the old lawbooks closely. Further, the widely-read author of *Njála* was very well acquainted with the Austfirðir but seems to have known nothing about *Hrafnkatla*; and this fact, according well with our saga's position in the development of saga literature,

Findings and Conclusions

suggests that it was composed at the same time as *Njála*, in the last quarter of the thirteenth century.

If we believe that the saga writer had any purpose in mind other than the desire to write a good novel, then one special point should be considered: the author is disposed to maintain that the Fljótsdæla-godord had been in the hands of the descendants of Hrafnkell from the very beginning of the settlement of Iceland. Unfortunately we have so little information contemporary with the saga's composition about the families and lives of those in power in the Austfirðir that, even if we believed this to be his purpose, it would be impossible to guess at any definite person as the author.

The time has now come to see if our researches into *Hrafnkatla* lead to any general conclusions about the Icelandic Family Sagas.

Though we have had no space here for any extensive comparison of *Hrafnkatla* with other sagas, we have tried to make it clear that all sagas must not be measured by one yardstick in respect of their historicity, their use of sources, or their artistic treatment of subject-matter. It is my opinion, many times confirmed, that each saga should receive its own independent and careful investigation. Although they all belong to one *genre* with clearly similar characteristics, yet an insight into the individual qualities of each saga is of primary importance, in order both to understand that saga better and to give a clearer picture of the *genre* as a whole and of the changes it underwent. It is as absurd and arbitrary to make all-embracing statements about the sagas after the examination of one saga as it is—and this is much more common—to frame a general theory about all the sagas and then apply it willy-nilly to works which are quite dissimilar.

Perhaps something may be learned, however, from these observations which may prove of value in investigating other Icelandic sagas. At least it has been my experience, ever since I first began to realize the nature and origins of this saga, that more and more I have been forced to abandon various notions which had been instilled into me since youth. Three of these deserve some consideration now.

1. Until the present time *Hrafnkatla* has been considered to be among the most reliable of sagas, and in some matters its evidence has been preferred even to that of *Landnáma*. Although the saga had not been the subject of special investigation, the following opinion was generally held and regarded as true: the saga was based on oral legend, therefore it must have had its roots in historical events; the saga was reliable except for a few trifling details, and this, in turn, demonstrated the trustworthiness of oral traditions as vehicles for conveying historical information. Then isolated details were tested in order to supply proofs of the saga's truthfulness, particularly by the study of the names of places and farms together with a little archaeology. For the most part such studies were based on faith and not on investigation; and even when investigation was undertaken, this too was based on trust (Hrafnkell's barrow) or made to fit the theory of the investigator (Freyfaxi's Bluff, &c.). If the premisses were generally of this type, what value can be placed on the general conclusions of scholars about the Icelandic sagas, when they erred so grievously in applying them to an individual saga? When from time to time I have indicated flaws and, indeed, nonsense in the writings of various scholars—even of Sigurður Vigfússon—it has not been done from any desire to belittle these worthy men. It has been done as a warning that much of the belief in the truthfulness of the Icelandic sagas is based on reasons which, if closely scrutinized, would turn out to be as untenable as those once used to support the veracity of *Hrafnkatla*.

2. Of all the Icelandic sagas *Hrafnkatla* seems to me to be the easiest to remember and to repeat for amusement. It has often been praised as an outstanding example of the art of oral saga. This can be tested easily by repeating our saga and then *Droplaugarsona saga*—which contains internal evidence to show that it was written from the narration of one man, however variously that evidence may be interpreted and debated—and thus trying to discover which saga is the easier to retell. After such an

Findings and Conclusions

experiment, will it seem preposterous to maintain that various qualities, which have been interpreted by our contemporaries as the best instances of oral recitation, are present in the sagas precisely because they were composed in the same way as *Hrafnkatla*: a written work of fiction so highly polished that in the very act of deceiving the reader it has assumed for him the 'platonic ideal' of what an orally transmitted story *ought* to be?

Finnur Jónsson has clearly recognized the excellence of *Hrafnkatla*: 'In respect of its composition the saga is a masterpiece, a spotless pearl among the Family Sagas', he says among other things. But later he adds this monstrous statement: 'Its composition prevents us from dating the saga any later than *c.* 1200. This is quite definite; it may easily be older than that.'[52] Now Finnur cannot avoid dating some sagas almost correctly. He was obliged to admit that the Kings' Sagas of Snorri were composed in the years 1225–35, that *Njála* in its present form could not have been composed before 1250–80; he places *Hænsa-Þóris saga* after 1250 or 1275, and *Grettis saga* around or after the year 1300. Yet *Hrafnkatla*, because of its masterly construction, cannot be later than 1200. The art of saga construction was no long understood when the above-mentioned sagas were written, not even at the time when Snorri was bungling the writing of his own sagas; in fact, the author of *Hrafnkatla* had to belong to the age of Oddr Snorrason and Gunnlaugr Leifsson! Must there be only one rule for evaluating the Icelandic sagas: in the beginning they were perfect, thereafter all was blemish and decay? Strangely enough some people have accepted this argument. When Heusler reckons that *Hrafnkatla* 'was in all probability written early' (see above) he has not much support for this opinion other than the literary histories of Finnur Jónsson and Mogk. And accepting Finnur Jónsson's view that the earlier a saga was written the better its construction, it was difficult to reach any other conclusion than Heusler's: that the sagas had received their complete artistic development in oral tradition. However logically they are argued, conclusions based on such doubtful premises must be inherently weak.

3. A general belief exists that it is easy to distinguish between the true Family Sagas (*Íslendingasǫgur*) and the frankly fictitious sagas (*Lygisǫgur*), that is between sagas which may have been based on ancient oral traditions and those which were fictions composed by the author. Lying sagas would give themselves away. They would be full of exaggerations and pointless accretions, unoriginal, with subject-matter drawn from widely scattered sources (from fairy stories, foreign tales of chivalry, classical legends, &c.). Their characterization would be stereotyped with all the characters cast in the same mould, sometimes unblemished angels, sometimes black demons. In direct contrast, one assumed that the writers of true Family Sagas shared a common purpose: to record nothing but what they believed to be right and true. But alas! the world suddenly ceased to produce such men 'about and after 1300'. If there were exceptions they were due to confused oral tradition such as we get in *Hænsa-Þóris saga*.[53] No decent man would set out to create a fictitious saga; nor indeed would he know how to do so properly! Now *Hrafnkatla* strongly suggests that Icelandic fictional literary art in the old days was not confined within these narrow limits of theory, and we must be ready to admit that in addition to those works which are manifestly poor works of fiction many more good sagas may also prove to have fictitious foundations. The old and well-tried touchstone has proved inadequate for the task of revealing how the sagas were made. Finnur Jónsson has argued for the truthfulness of *Gunnlaugs saga* in a very simple way; 'There are no grounds for not believing that the incidents here related are true in all essentials; *they are not inherently incredible.*'[54] But would not *Hrafnkatla*, too, pass all scrutiny on this very score and for the very same reason? All things considered, would it not be reckoned quite as credible and even more true to life than *Gunnlaugs saga*?

Strange though it may seem, it has so far been a thankless task at home in Iceland as well as among foreign scholars to call in question the historicity of the Icelandic sagas. But I believe that it is wrong to object to such investigations if they are made

Findings and Conclusions 63

with caution and do not go beyond what can be supported by reasonable proof. In particular there are two considerations which opponents of these researches should bear in mind.

The first of these might be called the attitude to sources. If we cease to believe that all the main incidents in the sagas are derived from oral tradition and that this tradition is generally reliable, then it follows that we must admit that we know less than we had supposed about the history, culture, and way of thinking of the Saga Age, and also less about the civilization which existed between the Saga Age and the time when the sagas were composed. For it is generally assumed that it was during the period between the Saga Age and the Age of Writing that such good work was done in preserving ancient folk-lengends and in sifting the material so garnered with masterly skill. If men are really concerned to find reliable sources for their knowledge of the Saga Age, then it is difficult to see what benefit they hope to derive from wilfully closing their eyes to reality, by refusing to recognize what is false as well as what is trustworthy evidence. Those who are anxious to believe everything play straight into the hands of those who wish to deny everything. Ari Thorgilsson talks about source-men whom he describes as students of truth and no liars. He seems to have known that men existed who were neither students of truth nor could they be relied upon to treat scrupulously what they had heard. 'Many believe what is false and suspect what is true', says the author of *Hrafns saga*. Just so: the one attitude leads to the other. We must learn therefore, as far as we can, to detect the false if we are concerned to prevent more reliable material from escaping our notice. And the old Icelandic culture will not suffer any loss even if we should find ourselves obliged to credit to authors of the thirteenth century some of the material for which we formerly thanked the saga-tellers of the eleventh or twelfth.

My second point does not reflect the interests of scholars; it is based on aesthetic considerations. Other things being equal, it is more pleasurable to read a story we believe to be true than a fictitious one. The masterly account of Grettir's fight with

Glámr in *Grettla* will be even more effective if we not only believe in ghosts but also believe that Grettir did wrestle with this particular spirit who was as potent as the saga says he was. It has been a point of honour with many to believe that the Icelanders in bygone days did actually distinguish themselves beyond other men exactly as the sagas report: that the youngster Bjǫrn Arngeirsson really did kill the champion Kaldimarr, and that Egill Skalla-Grímsson played an outstanding role in the battle of Vínheiðr. But are not Egill's exploits at Vínheiðr of small account compared with many other things that we know for a certainty he really did, if we can in fact interpret his poems and songs with tolerable accuracy? The saga-writer's characterization of Egill is in itself an intellectual feat, though it cannot be accepted in every detail as historical truth. Would it not be a very poor exchange to possess 'A true Account of the late Grettir Ásmundarson' in place of *Grettis saga*? Truth exists in many forms, and truth about the meaning of life itself is often more clearly displayed in fiction than in traditions or even in historical studies.

Although I can no longer trust it with my old simple faith, *Hrafnkatla* will always remain the same to me. Although he never lived at Hrafnkelsstaðir Hrafnkell is still as real a character in my eyes as Hamlet is—and Shakespeare, with equal absurdity, made *his* home at Elsinore. It is possible that all that *Landnáma* has to say about Thormóðr Thjóstarsson is accurate and true. But who, except for a few genealogists, would have cared at all about him had not two brothers been conceived for him in the brain of an artist in the eastern fjords of the country—two men who never existed but who, for all that, are immortal?

As for the honour of our nation, we must assert that on to the stage which will be left empty by the withdrawal from the pageant of history of so many fictitious killers and strong men from the Saga Age, a new kind of character will step forth from the wings where he has hitherto been hidden, the author of a saga. Is there any loss in such an exchange?[55] Surely it is an honour for Icelanders to have produced the men who wrote such books and

Findings and Conclusions

who knew what they were about when they composed them. I believe there is no example in the history of literature of men of such genius being rewarded for their labours with such ingratitude. Finnur Jónsson once fell into partial disgrace for referring to them daringly as 'authors', but he made amends with these words: 'When in this way one admits that oral tradition plays a leading part both in the content and in fixing the form—an admission I have always made—can one then really maintain *that the writing down, too, could have had any significance, that it could have been anything more than mere mechanical copying?*'[56] After this we are not surprised to read Paul V. Rubow saying, 'One can be astonished at the older Icelandic philogists' complete misconception of their forefathers' poetic genius and creative ability.'[57] I can agree wholeheartedly with these words of Rubow, although I disagree with many of his views about the age and origin of the Icelandic sagas as stated in his monograph.

Research into the subject-matter of the Icelandic sagas, which really began with Konrad Maurer's article on *Hænsa-Þóris saga*, was continued in the same spirit by Bjǫrn M. Ólsen (particularly in his article on *Gunnlaugs saga*) and is now at last being carried forward by the editors of *Hið íslenzk Fornritafélag*. Such research has always sailed between Scylla and Charybdis. On both sides there have been men eager to solve the problems by the simplest means. On the one hand we find a deep-rooted belief in the trustworthiness and merit of oral traditions; on the other, particularly in more recent times, a denial of the possibility that oral tradition could have preserved any kind of historical material for two or three centuries. Research of the kind which has been attempted here to test the truthfulness of *Hrafnkatla* must always prove a scandal to the Jews and appear as foolishness to the heathen: in the eyes of the believer an impious attack on something which ought to be defended and conserved as long as possible, while to the sceptics it must seem quite absurd to waste words in arguing a case in which, they know in advance, the evidence is fabricated. Still, since those stern judges, the historians, have not been able with their arguments to uproot these dreamlike fantasies about the oral sagas which are prevalent among some distinguished literary scholars, no one can call it a waste of time to investigate the problem more fully. Again, it is better to proceed by short steps than by big strides. In the introductions to the *Fornrit* editions rather more attention has been paid to the older views of the sagas, the views of the general public in Iceland and of scholars who place more emphasis on the oral tradition, than to the views of 'critical' historians. Those concerned with these editions were reared in the older belief: we are philologists and literary critics, not historians. The editions are intended primarily for the ordinary Icelander and, of necessity, will pay some attention to the state of his opinions. Most writing about the sagas has been in this spirit, and it would have been rash to make too clean a break with old ideas and conceptions. The consequence of this cautious conservatism has been twofold. First, those editions of the *Fornrit* which have appeared so far [1940] have generally laid too much stress on the part played by oral tradition in the subject-matter of the Family Sagas and on their historical value, while authors have not been given credit for more than was absolutely necessary. Secondly, too much attention has been devoted to antiquarian discussions in these editions while more fruitful fields of study have been left unexamined. Yet the older antiquarianism could not be uprooted without its place being taken by somewhat sounder research: *similia similibus*. At this stage in the discussion the urgent question is to claim a right to draw attention to the living core of the sagas, to free them from the chains of deep-rooted prejudice. This may be called a roundabout approach, but I prefer to regard it as an intermediate position in research, a halting-place which it is imprudent to pass by. A detour is sometimes preferable to a bog; it gets you through even though it takes longer. Other aims are still unattained: to assign the ancient sagas their rightful place in the many-sided development of our country; to explain as clearly as possible what their nature really is, since this must always be of supreme importance to an Icelander's knowledge of himself at all times; and, last but not

Findings and Conclusions

least, to distinguish clearly between the dross of the sagas and their living spirit: the mastery of style and method of narration, the character portrayal, the knowledge of men and their views on life. In brief, to teach men to read them with a deeper understanding and keener enjoyment. These objectives will not be lost sight of, although it will be the task of future generations to attack the steeper slopes which lead to them. After the detailed examination of many Icelandic sagas has shown more clearly their real nature, men will be able to set to work with greater courage. To some extent this monograph has profited by appearing in a form where there is more scope for giving freer expression to such ideas than in the introductions to the *Fornrit* editions. Still, it bears abundant traces of the difficulty of getting to the root of the problem in the present state of researches into the sagas. However, if I have made some contribution to the understanding of a small saga and have, in addition, helped to clarify somewhat the aims of those researches of which this is an example, then this monograph will not have been written in vain.

NOTES TO *HRAFNKATLA*

THESE notes are in the main those of Professor Nordal. Where the translator has added to them Professor Nordal's notes are followed by the initials (S.N.) and the translator's additions by (R.G.T.).

1. The full title of the saga is *Hrafnkels saga Freysgoða* but I have permitted myself to coin a diminutive of affection on the pattern of our common use of *Egla*, *Njála*, *Grettla*, and *Glúma*. I can quote by way of precedent the two manuscripts copied by Þorkell Jónsson, lǫgrettumaðr at Hraun in Grindavík, which have been named *Þorkatla* 'greater' and 'lesser'. (Catalogue numbers in the National Library of Iceland, Í.B. 633-4, 8vo.)

2. See *Hrafnkels saga Freysgoða*, edited by Frank Stenton Cawley, Cambridge, Mass., 1932, Preface, viii.

3. *Die Anfänge der isländischen Saga*, Berlin, 1914, pp. 61 and 84.

4. *Upphavet til den islendske ættesaga*, Copenhagen, 1929, pp. 121, 136.

5. *Transactions of the Philological Society*, 1931, pp. 32, 61. After this present monograph was finished I received a copy of E. V. Gordon's posthumous article now printed in *Medium Ævum*, viii, 1939. Sections of that article develop the same argument as is presented here, generally in a briefer form, and I have seen no reason to refer to it or to alter anything in my monograph because of it. It is obvious that E. V. Gordon's views on the Icelandic sagas had greatly changed between 1932 and 1938 when, to the irreparable loss of Icelandic studies in Britain, this learned and perceptive scholar died.

6. *Norges og Islands litteratur: indtil utgangen av middel alderen*, Oslo, 1924, pp. 330-1.

7. *Nordisk Kultur: VIII: B. Sagalitteraturen*, by Sigurður Nordal, Copenhagen, 1953, pp. 180-273 (R.G.T.).

8. For a discussion of the dating and composition of the older versions of *Landnámabók* I particularly wish to refer the reader to two monographs. One is by Bjǫrn M. Ólsen, *Ari Þorgilsson hinn fróði*, in *Tímarit*, 1889. The arguments there advanced in favour of Ari's authorship of *Landnáma* have never been disproved. Finnur Jónsson and various others have stubbornly refused either to endorse them or to disprove them. The other is by Barði Guðmundsson, *Uppruni Landnámabókar*, in *Skírnir*, 1938. By different lines of argument he reaches conclusions similar to those of Ólsen and adds some fresh reasons for accepting his view. (S.N.) Cf. Jón Jóhannesson, *Gerðir Landnámabókar*, Reykjavík, 1941, for a critical examination of *Landnáma* and its various versions. (R.G.T.)

Notes to Hrafnkatla

9. Let one example do duty for many. In his excellent book *Ættegaard og helligdom* Magnus Olsen makes this reference to our saga: 'Hrafnkell Freysgodi first lived at Aðalból but he had to leave that farm and settled at Hrafnkelsstaðir.' This statement has little value if Hrafnkell had lived neither at Aðalból nor at Hrafnkelsstaðir. In fairness one must add that although this single example is wrong, Olsen's general findings about the age of farms ending in *-staðir* are not invalidated. Instructive examples of the danger inherent in writing social (or cultural) histories of the early times and lumping together reliable and unreliable sources within the all-embracing term of 'saga-sources' may be found in Bernhard Kummer's *Midgards Untergang* and Helge Ljunberg's *Den nordiska religionen och kristendomen*.

10. Cf. 'Variant Readings of the Paper MSS. of *Hrafnkels saga Freysgoða*', by Randolph Quirk, *London Medieval Studies*, 1951. (R.G.T.)

11. The standard edition with variant readings is *Austfirðinga sǫgur*, edited by Jakob Jakobsen, Copenhagen, 1902–3. Since the saga is short I have not considered it necessary to refer on every occasion to chapter and page. (S.N.) The most recent editions are in *Austfirðinga sǫgur*, edited by Jón Jóhannesson, Íslenzk Fornrit XI, Reykjavík, 1950, in the Nordisk Filogi Text-Series (edited by Jón Helgason), Copenhagen, 1950, and Altnordische Textbibliothek, Neue Folge I, ed. by Walter Baetke, Halle, 1952. There is an admirable English translation of the saga in *Four Icelandic Sagas*, by Gwyn Jones (American Scandinavian Foundation), New York, 1935. (R.G.T.)

12. I have followed the example of Professor Gwyn Jones, op. cit., p. 135, in using the terms 'godi' and 'godord' for the untranslatable *goði* and *goðorð*. (R.G.T.)

13. See *Landnámabók*, edited by Finnur Jónsson, 1900.

14. The sources are not unanimous about these family relationships but the variations do not affect the case put forward here. See *Landnámabók*, edited by Finnur Jónsson, 1900, pp. 40 and 167; also the genealogies in *Geirmundar Þáttr Heljarskinns* [in *Sturlunga Saga* I, edited by Jón Jóhannesson, Reykjavík, 1946, p. 10. (R.G.T.)]; and *Safn til sǫgu Íslands*, iii. 514.

15. Ibid., i. 356; *Den oldnorske og oldislandske Litteraturs Historie*, ii (2nd edn., Copenhagen, 1923), p. 518.

16. *Landnámabók* (edition by F. Jónsson, 1925), chapter 375.

17. In this connexion we may ignore that son of Hallsteinn whom he sacrificed, according to the longer version of *Gísla saga*—a fact which also could have been deduced from *Landnáma*.

18. *Origines Islandicae*, edited by Vigfússon and Powell, Oxford, 1905, ii. 488–90.

19. Cf. E. H. Lind, *Norsk-isländska dopnamn och fingerade namn från medeltiden*. (Uppsala och Leipzig), 1905–15.

20. The index of names in editions of *Landnáma* wrongly assumes that this statement refers to Hrafnkell Thórisson. This may also be the source of Finnur Jónsson's observation, in his 1908 edition of *Brennu-Njálssaga*, that Hrafnkell Thórisson is the principal character in *Hrafnkatla*.

21. *Landnáma* frequently records the changes in the place of abode of settlers, even when they do not occur in the historic manner of Hrafnkell's move to Hrafnkelsstaðir. It is almost incredible that the source-men for the original settlement in this district could have known about this incident without mentioning it. If some traditions of this kind had existed, they must have sprung up later than the period when *Landnáma* was recorded.

22. Three of the four names given to the sons of Hrólfr and Hallsteinn belong to the sons of Sturla: Thórðr, Sighvatr, Snorri. Did the author unconsciously make use of these well-known names when he was christening his imaginary characters? This is only a guess, but it certainly is an odd coincidence.

23. See *Sturlunga saga*, edited by Kristian Kaalund, Copenhagen, 1906–11, ii. 205.

24. The name of the farm comes from its topography; cf. *halli* and *hallur* [a slope].

25. See the article by Ólafur Lárusson in *Skírnir*, 1935, p. 205.

26. Cf. *Austfirðinga sǫgur*, Íslenzk Fornrit XI, pp. xlii–xliii. (R.G.T.)

27. *Hallfreðargata* is still known and the name is hardly the invention of the author, even though his description is inaccurate. Cf. *Safn til sǫgu Íslands* ii. 454, where it is pointed out that in chapter 2 of the saga *Fljótsdalsheiði* ought to stand for *Fljótsdalsheraði*. The same error occurs twice later in the saga, in the description of Hrafnkell's ride to the Thing and in the account of his departure from Aðalból. It is more likely that these are copyists' errors than that they are mistakes by the author.

28. *Torfa* seems to me to be incapable of direct translation into English. In those parts of Iceland where there is considerable soil-erosion due to wind and sand the turf was often under-cut in such a way as to leave islands of soil topped with turf; in between these islands were deep channels surfaced with rock or sand. These islands were called *torfa* and some of them were fairly large. The South Wales dialect word 'tump' (cf. Buttington Tump) applies to the shape but not to the nature of these *torfa*. I must thank Mr. Benedikt Benedikz for helping to clarify this point for me. (R.G.T.)

29. *Árbók Fornleifa-félagsins*, 1893, p. 37.

Notes to Hrafnkatla

30. It is difficult to believe that Sámr would have erected a barrow for his brother on a wind-swept *torfa* when it was perfectly obvious that the barrow would be blown away and the bones scattered. But it is not necessary to accept such an interpretation from the words of the saga.

31. *Fljótsdæla saga* has taken over the name directly from *Hrafnkatla*. (S.N.) '*Aðalból*' occurs three times in this sixteenth-century saga; see Íslenzk Fornrit XI, pp. 216, 218, and 238. (R.G.T.)

32. Jón Jóhannesson [late Professor of History in the University of Iceland] informed me of this. (In the index to Diplomatarium Islandicorum IV, Laugarhús is inadvertently recorded in Fnjóskadalr.) He also described to me some of the deserted saga-farms which I have not had the opportunity to visit myself. For the rest, however, the saga-author's personal acquaintance with places mentioned in *Hrafnkatla* has little or no bearing on the main thesis of this monograph.

33. Dr. Páll Eggert Ólason has given me the following account of the history of the dale:

Hrafnkelsdalr had long been the property of the church at Valthjófsstaðir in Fljótsdalr. The evidence for this is in Diplomatarium Islandicorum XII under 15 May 1552. (From this reference one can only deduce that the dale was then completely uninhabited.) There was, according to this evidence, a court ruling later in 1621 which is not now extant, but evidence of its existence and of the evidence submitted in 1552 can be found in the visitation of Bishop Brynjólfur, 1641. The 1696 Rent-roll gives these particulars for Hrafnkelsdalr in the parish of Brúarthing: assessment, '6 hundred', ground rent '60 *álnir*', value in cows '1'; but the dale is not included in later rent-rolls and there is no later mention of a farm with this name. In the first parish register from Valthjófsstaðir, in 1783, there is mention of 'Vaðbrekka í Rafnkelsdal' and of 'Aðalból í Rafnkelsdal', which were in the parish of Valthjófsstaðir and naturally belonged to the church there. Later, both these farms were brought under the parish of Brú. Neither of these farms is mentioned in any Rent-roll before 1804; possibly they were listed as new farms in accordance with the Provisions for New Farms, 1776. In the church documents for Valthjófsstaðir the assessments for Aðalból and Vaðbrekka are regularly given from 1824. From that document it can be shown that there was in Hrafnkelsdalr a deserted farm called Þórisstaðir. (Cf. *Árbók Fornleifafélagsins*, 1893, pp. 37–38.)

34. Matthías Þórðarson, Keeper of the Icelandic National Museum, has been kind enough to give me a report on these bones. From it the reader can decide for himself the probability of Sigurður's having discovered Hrafnkell's place of burial. Here are Matthías Þórðarson's observations (in a letter to me):

In accordance with your request I have re-examined the bones which Sigurður Vigfússon dug up on 11 July 1890 from 'a burial ground which was about 80 fathoms away from Aðalból in Hrafnkelsdalr.' They are exhibits Nos. 3466 and 3467; about 20 decayed fragments of wood which he found with the bones constitute exhibit No. 3468. He declares these to have been added to the collection on 4 September of the same year, does not enter the addition in the Museum's Logbook, but refers to it in his personal diary of the investigations which is printed on pages 39-42 of the *Árbók Fornleifafélagsins* 1893. However, he has recorded in the Museum's Logbook that the bones No. 3466 are those of 'Hrafnkell Freysgoði'. Judging from size I think that No. 3466 are more likely to be the bones of a female. The person from whom they came could not have been taller than 166 cm. [5 ft. 5 in.]; they are all rather thin, the skull is rather small, and the front teeth which are with the bones are also small. The teeth indicate that this person was about fifty at the time of death. No. 3467 are thicker and seem to be those of a man, but a very short one, and the remnants of the jawbone suggest that he was very old at the time of death. It can be seen from Sigurður's report that he believed that the scraps of wood which he found with the body were 'scorched by fire on the outside', and he deduced that 'burned wood had been strewn over the body'. The wooden fragments which now form exhibit No. 3468 bear no trace of burning or scorching and the dark colouring still observable on them is the normal result of burying any kind of wood in the earth for a long period of time.

S.V. found no objects with the bones which could have given some indication of the date or the sex of the buried persons, but the position in the ground of the bones No. 3466, lying from north to south, indicated that they must have been from pagan times. Sigurður states that he found 'iron mould and green mould' with the bones; this suggests that articles of iron and copper or bronze had been buried with the bodies, and that is another thing to indicate that they had been buried in heathen times ... Sigurður believed that the 'barrow' in which he found these bones had been 'somewhat disturbed later', i.e. long after the people were buried, and this is not unlikely since he also says that the bones No. 3467 had been 'scattered'. The other skeleton, No. 3466, which I believe to be that of a woman, seems to have been placed normally in the earth, which indicates that it had not been disturbed nor had any weapon been taken from it ... The most curious feature of this discovery of bones near Aðalból is the discovery of the fragments of wood; S.V. states that they 'were placed upon the bodies from above' when they were interred. This type of covering has not been found in any other graves or barrow burials, but it would not be safe to conclude from this that the barrow burial under discussion must be later than, or from, Christian times, since Hrafnkelsdalr was settled and inhabited 'late in the period of settlement.'

Notes to Hrafnkatla

35. So Jón Jóhannesson, who has examined the site, tells me.

36. One manuscript of the saga, which Jakobsen calls D, is sometimes more detailed in its description of places than the others, which suggests that at some later date one person thought the saga-author's knowledge deficient.

37. Ólafur Briem has drawn my attention to this.

38. Jacob Jakobsen considers that *Hrafnkatla* is more trustworthy than *Landnáma inter alia* 'because *Landnáma* seems to know nothing of Hrafnkell's nickname—at least it makes no mention of it; a nickname, moreover, which is so securely founded in the important part which Frey-worship plays in *Hrafnkelssaga* and to which the place-name Freyfaxahamarr, called after Hrafnkell's horse dedicated to Frey, bears witness'. (*Austfirðinga sǫgur*, p. l) Here it is first assumed that everything which is said about Hrafnkell's Frey-worship is true, and subsequently that assumption is used to support the truth of the saga against *Landnáma*. No account is taken of the argument that *Hrafnkatla*, which is the only ancient source for Freyfaxahamarr, gives a wrong description of the place, if Hrafnkell had lived at Aðalból. On the basis of such circular reasoning *Landnáma* is set aside.

39. One such incident, which took place in 1879, about the personal mount of Hjǫrtur bondi in Austurhlið, is printed in *Lǫgberg*, vol. 49, no. 1. Its similarity to the story of Freyfaxi is astonishing, for it is an eye-witness account supported with such exact detail that it is difficult to doubt it.

40. In Jakobsen's edition (p. 127) the period is given as '7 years' in all manuscripts except one; later, on p. 135, the period is given as '6 years'. The figure 6 should have been used on both occasions, but the error must have arisen because immediately afterwards the text states that Eyvindr had been abroad 7 years; yet he had left the country before the slaying of Einarr.

41. See *Three Icelandic Sagas*, translated by M. Schlauch and M. H. Scargill, Princeton U.P. for the American Scandinavian Foundation, 1950. (R.G.T.)

42. *Gesta Danorum*, liber viii.

43. See *Origines Islandicae*, ii. 491.

44. Compare my book *Snorri Sturluson* (Reykjavík, 1920) where a few examples of this are given on pp. 130, 135, 147–8, 150.

45. There is a monograph which I have not been able to see (by Otto Opet) on the legal knowledge displayed in *Hrafnkatla*. For the most part I can ignore the subject here. The saga-writer is mistaken in allowing the lawsuit for Einarr's slaying to go direct to the Althing.

He talks about the court sitting on the Lǫgberg. Here surely is negligence, not ignorance: *dómar fóru út frá Lǫgbergi* and then the case for the slaying was announced there. This has certainly been confused. A misinterpretation of the godi's power (*mannaforráð*) is shown in the words: *Lagði hann (Hrafnkell) land undir sik allt fyrir austan Lagarfljót.* I do not know what Finnur Jónsson could have meant by saying that *Hrafnkatla* 'contains various important statements' about law and judicial procedure.

46. My count gives them 42 per cent. of the saga. As a basis for comparison here are some other percentages; *Bandamanna saga* 55, *Valla-Ljóts saga* 46–47, *Hænsa-Þóris saga* 39, *Gunnlaugs saga* 28, *Reykdæla saga* 6–7. These figures are taken from the Icelandic edition of Knut Liestøl's book, *Uppruni Íslendinga sagna*, Reykjavík, 1938, p. 74.

47. The meaning of this phrase has caused some difficulty. The general meaning is clear: Eyvindr's page advises him to flee: 'if you escape there is nothing at stake, no very great risk, no matter what happens to us'. *Festr* here has been explained as 'a trap' (cf. Cawley's edition, cited above), but there is no other example of this meaning. It is possible that *festr* could be translated as either 'trap' or 'deadlock' It has occurred to me that *dýr* may stand for *dýrgripr* ('treasure, precious thing') as Axel Koch explains the word in *Vǫlundarkviða* (*Arkiv for nordisk filologi*, xxvii. 107), and I have also found the same word in one verse of Kormákr (*skoglar dýr*: good weapon; cf. Íslenzk Fornrit VIII. p. 240). This phrase, then, may be very old.

48. 'The style is hardly on a par with the composition'; *Litteraturs historie*, ii, ed. cit., p. 516.

49. I have omitted the following sentences from Professor Nordal's text at this point: 'Who can ignore the progress made in style and taste by Icelanders during the period 1750–1850? Though we could not date the *Brandur* of Bishop Geir Víðalín solely by comparing its style to that of *Minnisverð Tíðindi* or Tómas Sæmundsson's essays by the linguistic usages of his contemporaries Jónas Hallgrímsson and Konráð Gíslason.' (R.G.T.)

50. Explained in greater detail in my *Snorri Sturluson*, pp. 217–19.

51. This quotation is from Knút Liestøl, *Uppruni Íslendinga sagna*, ed. cit., pp. 75–76 (S.N.) Sir Walter Scott, *The Abbot*, The Waverley Novels, XI, London, 1900, pp. 5–6. (R.G.T.)

52. *Litteraturs historie*, ii. 516–17.

53. In my introduction to this saga (Íslenzk Fornrit III, Reykjavík, 1938) I have shown that its author deliberately deviated from *Íslendingabók* as our author does from *Landnáma*.

54. *Litteraturs historie* ii. 415: my italics.

Notes to Hrafnkatla

55. I have omitted the following sentence here: ' "Size and strength go far and wide. But wisdom still must be their guide", says Páll Viðalín the Lawman.' (R.G.T.)

56. *Litteraturs historie*, ii. 206–7: my italics.

57. *Smaa kritiske breve*, ii. (S.N.) Cf. Paul V. Rubow, *Two Essays*, Copenhagen, 1949, pp. 30–64. (R.G.T.)

PRINTED IN
GREAT BRITAIN
AT THE
UNIVERSITY PRESS
OXFORD
BY
CHARLES BATEY
PRINTER
TO THE
UNIVERSITY